AN INTRODUCTION TO THEOLOGICAL RESEARCH

A Guide for College and Seminary Students

Second Edition, Revised and Expanded

D0840217

AN INTRODUCTION TO THEOLOGICAL RESEARCH

A Guide for College and Seminary Students

Second Edition, Revised and Expanded

Cyril J. Barber
Robert M. Krauss, Jr.

Foreword by

J. P. Moreland

University Press of America, ® Inc.
Lanham • New York • Oxford

Copyright © 2000 by
University Press of America, ® Inc.
4720 Boston Way
Lanham, Maryland 20706

12 Hid's Copse Rd.
Cumnor Hill, Oxford OX2 9JJ

Library of Congress Cataloging-in-Publication Data

Barber, Cyril J.
An introduction to theological research : a guide for college and
seminary students / Cyril J. Barber, Robert M. Krauss, Jr. ;
foreword by J. P. Moreland.—2nd ed.
p.   cm.
Includes bibliographical references and index..
l. Theology—Research. I. Krauss, Robert M. II. Title.
BR118.B28   2000   230'.07'2—dc21   00-023378 CIP

ISBN 0-7618-1659-3 (pbk: alk. ppr.)

4 3615328

Table of Contents

Foreword

To the Second Edition by
J. P. Moreland

The evangelical community finds itself in an odd position today. On the one hand, our numbers are strong if measured by the overall population of the United States, churches continue to be planted, and evangelical publishing, radio and so forth show no sign of weakening. On the other hand, our impact is quite small in comparison to our numbers, the public discourse of our culture continues to grow more and more secular and post-Christian, the make up man is more important than the speech writer in our political process, and evangelical Christianity is mired in marginalization at the edges of cultural influence.

What is going on here? In my view, we evangelicals are simply not producing intelligent, articulate, winsome leaders who have the spiritual power and intellectual training to outlive and outthink those outside the church. We live in what is most likely the most anti-intellectual period in the history of Christianity and there is growing pressure on seminary students, ministers, and Christian teachers generally to adopt a shallow, popularistic approach to teaching, preaching, and ministry. But we Christians must resist this trend and refuse to give slogans instead of answers, sound-byte messages instead of well-reasoned expressions of our views, simplistic books and articles instead of meaty food for God's people. We must equip God's people to think and study for themselves instead of simply filling their spiritual tanks each week with the result that they become inordinately dependent upon the teacher to tell them what to believe.

This is why the publication of this new edition of *An Introduction to Theological Research* by Barber and Krauss is so timely. Christian leaders, lay and professional alike, must do their homework, and research is the only way to do that. It is my hope that this book will become a standard tool in every Christian leader's library and that it will be a valuable guide and time-saver to all those who have the responsibility of teaching, preaching, and representing Christ in the arena of ideas. This new edition retains what was valuable in the first edition, but it is thoroughly updated and expanded, including new information about the use of electronic databases and the Internet. May God use this book to help Christian leaders and teachers be more articulate, effective stewards of the manifold wisdom of God.

Foreword

To the First Edition by
Walter C. Kaiser, Jr.

Easily one half of an education in any discipline in the humanities, such as biblical or theological studies, consists of knowing where to turn for the proper tools and how to use them once they are located. Professor Cyril Barber has opened these doors for us.

This volume had its origins in a course that the author prepared while he was librarian at Trinity Evangelical Divinity School. That course, entitled "Theological Research Methods," was designed to help master of arts and master of theology students gain bibliographic control over the whole range of theological literature while they prepared to investigate a selected topic for a graduate level thesis.

Many of these same procedures and principles of research are modified in this volume to provide the broadest foundation for the largest number of students of the Scriptures. Any student of the Bible who loves to explore its text and the various theological disciplines will bristle with delight as he or she is led by this master bibliographer and bibliophile through illuminating descriptions on the general and specific reference tools. Especially useful will be the discussions of concordances, the importance of lexicons, and the chapters on word studies.

Professor Barber has rightly earned a reputation as the evangelical Nestor of basic bibliography for minister's libraries. In fact, his magnum opus in this area, *The Minister's Library*, was published in 1974. It has been kept up-to-date with periodic supplements and cumulations, each of which maintains an annotated format and the eleven major divisions used in the first volume.

Therefore, it is a pleasure to commend Cyril Barber's *An Introduction to Theological Research: A Guide for College and Seminary Students* to all who truly aspire to enter into biblical and theological studies as fully as possible, given the tools at their disposal. Anyone who spends even a few hours with this guide will be richly repaid in many more profitable hours of happy research. Furthermore, we believe that the ministry of those researchers, whether they be behind the classroom lectern, the congregational pulpit, or the scholarly pen, will be markedly more effective and penetrating. Their ministry will also be more alert to the issues involved in a given subject, the history of the discussion that has ensued, and the advantages that have been achieved. Theological research need not be thought of as exotic or the domain of a few gifted academicians; rather it is as ordinary and available as most of the books mentioned in these pages.

Preface

by Cyril J. Barber

I am deeply grateful for the reception given the first edition of this book. It became popular with faculty members as well as students, and reviewers were generally kind in their comments. In the course of time, however, it became dated and my busy schedule left me no time to revise it. The project, therefore, had to be delayed until after I had finished writing commentaries on *The Books of Kings*. During all this time online searching of electronic databases had become a specialized field in its own right, and I realized that I needed the help of a specialist to make a revision of *An Introduction to Theological Research* truly viable.

I had volunteered my services at the Biola library reference desk one night a week, and this afforded me the opportunity of working closely with Robert M. Krauss, Jr. (a former Chaplain, Lt. Colonel in the United States Air Force). It was during these evenings that I came to realize that Bob Krauss' background and training (including degrees in theology; marriage, family and child counseling; and library and information science) admirably equipped him as a research specialist. And his illustrious career has demonstrated over and over again that he does not believe in half-measures. To my great joy he agreed to collaborate with me on the second edition of this work.

Bob joins me in thanking Dr. J. P. Moreland of Biola University for so kindly reading the manuscript and writing the foreword.

Acknowledgements

The authors gratefully acknowledge the permission to quote from the following works:

To the Review and Herald Publishing Association for permission to quote from *I Love Books* by J.D. Snyder.

To Charles C. Ryrie for permission to quote from the notes of the *Ryrie Study Bible*.

To the University of Chicago Press for permission to quote from *Letters From Mesopotamia*, translated and with an introduction by A Leo Oppenheim.

To the Zondervan Publishing House for permission to quote from the *New International Dictionary of New Testament Theology*, edited by C. Brown.

1

Introduction

Is there a need for this book? Isn't the curriculum full enough without adding another course?

There was a time when only the best schools paid any serious attention to research. Now many Bible and Christian liberal arts colleges as well as seminaries require all their students to take a course in theological research with an emphasis in online databases. And the reason? An unprecedented knowledge explosion. The situation we face can best be described in linear terms. If, for example, we could measure knowledge in inches, the amount of knowledge known to man since the dawn of time to 1845 would equal about one inch. In the century from 1845 to 1945 (i.e., the end of World War II), it would have tripled to three inches. Then, from 1945 to 1970 knowledge multiplied at a phenomenal rate so that if we continued to apply a linear measure to this era, the amount of data would have exceeded the height of the Washington Monument. And since then information has been proliferating so rapidly it doubles every seven years.

Now, according to Dr. Charles Vest, president of the Massachusetts Institute of Technology, "huge amounts of information" proliferate at such a rapid rate so that "scientific and technical knowledge doubles every three to five years."[1]

In the past, the prerequisites of a good education were the faculty under whom one studied and the library in which one pursued his or her research. Today, however, a new dimension must be added: guidance in the use of electronic databases and the Internet. Traditionally, instruction in these areas is being done by librarians who are no longer guardians of the books, but information specialists acting as guides into the world of knowledge. And the library now serves as a gateway to a world of enlightenment that was unthought of two or three decades ago.

But there's more. The "information explosion" can no longer be confined to data that can be stored in one building or even in several buildings. Institutions are now dependent upon one another, and resource sharing among libraries is a necessity. Interlibrary loan has experienced a phenomenal growth during the last decade. And don't be surprised when you discover that libraries provide Internet access to information scattered throughout the world, and that you can have full text copies of articles from thousands of different journals displayed on your computer screen.

Now, about this time, you may be feeling a little overwhelmed. Rest assured of the fact that this will pass. We will show you how to use the library effectively. You can expect your level of confidence to increase after your initial contact with FirstSearch, ProQuest, EBSCOhost, SilverPlatter, or Eureka or any one of a plethora of electronic databases. As you use these resources your initial impression may he one of not knowing how to separate the "wheat' from the "chaff." For your encouragement, we will try to make your learning experience as painless as possible. We will also confine ourselves to a few of the more important resources of information.

As we describe each research tool, we will make specific comments on its strengths and weaknesses. Not all the works are of equal value. Their usefulness will largely be dependent upon your specific needs as well as the subject you are researching. Our purpose will be to eliminate as far as possible what William Wordsworth referred to as the "gloom of uninspired research." The best way to do this is to facilitate the collection of data. By knowing where to go for the information you need, you will be in the enviable position of having more data at your fingertips than you can use in your paper or thesis or dissertation. It is always easier to narrow your field or eliminate superfluous information than it is to try and expand some poorly researched project to meet the requirements of an exacting professor. By following the suggestions contained in this book the result should be qualitatively better work and a greater sense of personal fulfillment.

One word of counsel: At no time should you feel that you are required to believe all you read. What you find in books and journal articles and on the Internet should be read with discernment. And though theological liberals may deny the fundamental doctrines of Christianity, we all can learn much from their writings. Furthermore, this can be done without compromising any of our convictions, for it is the Holy Spirit Himself who guides us into all truth (John 8:32; 16:13; 17:17*b*).

In preparing this book we kept a record of the kinds of questions asked us. Several busy evenings yielded the following:

- Within a few months of the world being awakened to the significance of the papyrus fragments now known as the Magdalen Papyrus, a student came to the reference desk with a question: One of my professors mentioned the 'Magdalen Papyrus' in class today, and I have decided to write a paper on it for the course I'm taking. I've consulted the library catalog, but haven't been able to find any references to it. I shall appreciate any help you can give me!

- Our evangelism class has been told to research the question, 'Does conversion involve the Lordship of Christ?' for a debate next Wednesday. We are required to know who are the leading advocates, and what has been written by or about them.

- I'm doing a paper on the two natures of Christ for a Christology course. I've checked the library's catalog but cannot find any references to my topic. Does the library have any books on Christology?

- In 'The History of Christian Thought' course I'm taking we've been told to familiarize ourselves with the beliefs and practices of the Arians, Monophosites, Montanists, and Nestorians. In which source or sources am I most likely to find this kind of information?

- I'm a Christian Ed. major. My professor thought it would be a good idea if each person in the class surveyed ten years of articles in a religious journal to observe different trends. He told us to avoid magazines. How does a journal differ from a magazine? And what journals can you recommend in my area?

- We have a major paper due in two weeks on the 'Baptism of [2]the Holy Spirit.' How does one go about researching this topic?

- In our class for pastor's wives, we've been assigned a major term paper on the feminine attributes of God. It's worth half our grade. My husband has shown me the major systematic theologies, and I've consulted the usual indexes and abstracts. So far I've failed to find any information. Can you help me?

- In our missions class we've each been assigned a different religious movement. We are to research the movement and then present our findings in class. We're also required to type up our paper and give a copy to each person in the class. My topic is the 'Schwenkfelders.' I've never heard of them before. Where will I find information about them?

- I've been ill and missed the first week of class. Now I've a lot of catching up to do. Our homiletics instructor has assigned us Bible characters to preach on. Mine is Balaam. He stressed the importance of finding out all that the Bible has to say on a particular character before beginning our study for sometimes something in the New Testament will highlight an incident in the Old. Apart from the Book of Numbers, where will I find other references to Balaam in the Bible?

- In Greek 303 we've been assigned a word study on *apostasia*. At first I thought this would be easy. I've consulted *TDNT* only to find that this word is not treated. What should I do?

Does this sound familiar? These are the typical kinds of questions asked every day by students in the regular course of their research. Such questions invariably come after much abortive searching and are frequently accompanied by evidence of frustration and some embarrassment. Students, it seems, feel they should know where to find all sorts of information, or they assume that they should be computer-literate with a knowledge of a variety of Internet search engines and databases in all fields of inquiry. They also fear that to ask a librarian for help is to tacitly admit failure. Such a view is definitely not true. Most reference librarians are only too willing to help! We have assisted students who had spent many hours searching for information that could be found in a few minutes.

Our aim in preparing this book is to introduce students to the process of research that will result in lifelong learning. In preparing this material we have been guided by three basic objectives:

1. Our desire to reduce each student's research time to about one-tenth of what he or she would normally spend looking for information;

2. Our desire to enable each student to gain access to the kind of data that will help him or her produce qualitatively better papers (or thesis or dissertation, as the case may be); and

3. Our desire to make each student happily independent of our services.

In this last area we have been guided by the mature wisdom of Elbert Hubbard, who wrote: "The object of teaching is to enable the student to get along without his [or her] teacher." To this can be added the statement attributed to William Fowler: "An education isn't how much you have committed to memory, or even how much you know. It's being able to differentiate between what you know and what you don't. It's knowing where to go to find out what you need to know; and it's knowing how to use the information you get."

Hindsight has shown that those students who took the time to master a few techniques in the use of printed resources, the Internet, and various

CD-ROMs, experienced a greater sense of fulfillment as they pursued their studies. They also did better work even in subject areas that were of little interest to them. And as they gained experience, they became possessed of a confidence they had never known before.

In dealing with the needs of today's students, we need to reiterate an important point. As we begin, we will do so from the premise that you have little or no knowledge of a specific topic assigned you by one of your professors. The place to begin, therefore, is with general reference works. These resources will give you an overview of the material. Then, once this information has been mastered, it will be comparatively easy for you to move on to specific resources as you gather additional data. In other words, task number one is to become familiar with a few proven general reference works--e.g., Bible encyclopedias, Bible dictionaries, etc.—that are designed by their arrangement and treatment to be consulted for definite items of information, rather than to be read consecutively. By means of these resources you will be able to gain an overview of the subject you are researching. Then, once you have defined the parameters of your topic, you can enlarge your understanding by reading more specialized monographs. This done you will be in a position to read with greater understanding the kind of information contained in journal articles.

As you begin to evaluate general reference works, you should focus on the following specifics: accuracy, authority, scope, currency of the information, arrangement (including ease of use), and special features.

Accuracy, of course, is the single most important characteristic, and this applies to older works as well as more recent ones. Indexing is also an asset to the researcher. Documentation of sources cited or places where additional information can be found are likewise a plus. Then ascertain how comprehensive the discussion is. Does the presentation have any uniqueness (personal experience or eyewitness accounts of the writer). What is the format? How are the data organized? And how current is it?

As you begin to gather data, you should:

- Take note of the writer's outline and observe how he or she proceeds with the unfolding of the subject matter or deals with specifics that pertain to the topic under consideration.

- Learn about those who have contributed in one way or another to the body of knowledge that has grown up around your subject.

- Plot your topic's historic development.

- Ascertain the limitations and scope of your topic.

- Check the bibliography at the end of the article. See if it is impartial (i.e., presents both sides of the issue). Learn the representative works in this area of study and when these contributions were made. Which of these books is most likely to give you the help you seek?

Now, spend time examining the article on "Abraham" in *Zondervan Pictorial Encyclopedia of the Bible.* Trace the early history of the family from antediluvian times to the era of the patriarch. Check the bibliography at the end of the article. Does it contain the kind of works to which you might profitably refer if you were researching the life of this "father" of the faithful?

Remember that truth is timeless. "Research" is not to assume that the latest information is, *ipso facto,* all that you will need. The Cambridge University professor, T. R. Glover, in his book *Jesus in the Experience of Men,* wrote:

> The minds of most of us are like palimpsests, written over and over again; here the latest notion stands out in the newest script, but between the letters are to be found traces of ideas much older, obliterated but legible; there the oldest is almost untouched, but the closer observer finds hints of a "later hand." Every great thinker sets men writing these palimpsests.[3]

And C. S. Lewis, during his years at Oxford University, when he wrote his *Screwtape Letters,* warned:

> A new book is still on trial, and an amateur is not in a position to judge it. It has to be tested against the great body of Christian thought down through the ages, and all its hidden implications (often unsuspected by the author himself) have to be brought to light. Often it cannot be fully understood without the knowledge of a good many other books.... It is a good rule, after reading a new book, never to allow yourself another new one till you have read an old one in between.[4]

"But," someone will ask, "does this system of first researching general reference works (to find out what happened, and when, and where, while also ascertaining who the prime movers were) really work?"

Consider the situation of Stephen. He was a computer science major and found himself compelled to take a history course to round out his program. The only one scheduled at a convenient time (that would not conflict with his other classes) was Medieval History. So, to make a long story longer, he signed up for it. Imagine his surprise when, on the first day of class, his professor told him that he had to write a paper on "The History of Banking in Baghdad in the Eighth Century." The results of his research had to be presented to the class in three weeks.

Stephen consulted several online databases and the Internet, but without success. With ill-disguised disgust he came to the reference desk and asked for help. But where does one begin to find this kind of information? The usual indexes did not turn up a single reference to banking practices in Baghdad.

"Stephen," we said, "it has generally been found to be a good policy to check reference works first, and then proceed on to specialized monographs."

So we suggested a few secular encyclopedias that he might wish to consult.

A short time later a jubilant Stephen came back. His smile spoke volumes. He admitted that he had been skeptical of our suggestion. However, lacking any other viable plan of action, he decided to humor us and do as we had recommended. In one encyclopedia he had checked under "Banking, History of" and to his astonishment had found some information pertinent to his paper. More importantly, the bibliography at the end of the article listed an essay: "Banking in 8th Century Baghdad," published by the Royal Asiatic Society. On checking further he found that two California libraries listed this journal in their holdings.

Stephen filled out an interlibrary loan form, and received a copy of the article about a week later. Furthermore, from the bibliography at the end of the article he was able to trace other important leads to viable information.

The point that we wish to make is this: The essence of bibliographic research is knowing where to find the information you need. And it is our goal in this book to help you broaden your awareness of reference materials—both print and electronic—so that you can get off to a good start without wasting valuable time.

Of course, an introductory book such as this one must have certain limitations. Instead of covering the literally hundreds (and perhaps thousands) of reference works available today, we will concentrate on only a few (in reality, only those that experience has shown to be most valuable). Those desiring a more comprehensive approach are referred to the following sources of additional information: Gorman and Gorman's *Theological and Religious Reference Materials,* Johnston's *Recent Reference Books in Religion*, Kepple and Muether's *Reference Works for Theological Research*, and Thomas Mann's *The Oxford Guide to Library Research*. Of a more specialized nature, and to illustrate the growing number of bibliographies in different disciplines, there is Bradley and Muller's *Church History: An Introduction to Research, Reference Works, and Methods*.

In order to assist you understand what we will be doing in the remainder of this book, let us lay out our approach. We will begin with general reference tools and then move to specialized resources.

General Reference Works	**Special Resource Tools**
Bible encyclopedias	Books, monographs
Bible dictionaries	Periodical databases
Atlases	Electronic resources
Concordances	Bibliographies
	Unpublished materials

Initially, we will look at those *general* reference works that will give you an overview of the topic or subject to be researched. You will either have chosen the topic or it will have been assigned to you. These general reference works will lay a foundation for more specific investigation later on. *Special* resource tools will include those comprehensive guides to books, journals, and unpublished theses or dissertations that will enrich your study and broaden your horizons while also adding depth and insight to your understanding of the topic under consideration. The key is to move from the general to the specific!

Once you have learned the art of research, you should be able to find almost anything.

LOOKING AHEAD

Each chapter of this book will conclude with an assignment. The purpose of the assignment is to enable you to become familiar with the sources of information. In preparation for the next chapter it will be helpful for you to examine certain general reference works to ascertain their strengths and weaknesses, theological biases, and abiding values. You will look first at the broad area of religious reference tools and then narrow the field to Bible encyclopedias and dictionaries. You will probably find the books listed below in the reference section of your library.

In the rush to use electronic resources there is a danger that the rich heritage of the past will be lost. So that you will not suffer such a loss, we will begin with:

Hastings' Encyclopedia of Religion and Ethics

M'Clintock and Strong's *Cyclopedia of Biblical, Theological and Ecclesiastical Literature*

New Schaff-Herzog Encyclopedia of Religious Knowledge

New Unger's Bible Dictionary

Hastings' *Dictionary of the Bible*

International Standard Bible Encyclopedia

Interpreter's Dictionary of the Bible

Zondervan Pictorial Encyclopedia of the Bible

For the sake of comparison you may wish to consult articles on such varied topics as "Baptism," "Ethics," "Marriage," "Prayer," "Titus, Epistle of," and Zwingli."

In sharpening your skills, and at the same time determining the value of each work, consider carefully the following five points:

1. What is the nature and scope of each of these works (this is generally spelled out in the Introduction or the Preface)? How does this encyclopedia or dictionary differ from its predecessors? How comprehensive is it? Can you discern any strengths or weaknesses? Has it undergone revision (see the reverse of the title page)? Then check on (a) the editor(s), and (b) the contributors (a list of the contributors will often be found either in volume 1 or among the indices in the last volume).

   For writers from the era of the church Fathers to the present you may wish to consult Earle Cairn's *Wycliffe Biographical Dictionary of the Church*, the 1982 revised and enlarged edition of Elgin S. Moyer's *Who Was Who in Church History*. It is quite possibly the most accurate work of its kind. You may also wish to read corresponding articles in the *New International Dictionary of the Christian Church*, *Who's Who in Christian History*, or *Twentieth Century Dictionary of Christian Biography* edited by J. D. Douglas. (More will be said of these resources later on in this book.)

   Does an awareness of the theological training and denominational affiliation of the editor(s) and contributors give any indication (a) of the theological slant of each work, and (b) the level of scholarship to be expected?

2. As you focus attention on specific articles (e.g., "grace," "marriage," "prayer," etc.), pay special attention to the outline (if any). How did the writer approach his/her topic (analytically, historically, topically, or some other way)? Does the article contain "See" or "See also" references either within the body of the text or at the end? Has the writer used any documentation (e.g., Scriptural references or citations from other writers)? How pertinent are these references?

3. How extensive is the bibliography? Is it truly representative (i.e., presenting all sides of the issue)? Which works cited do you feel warrant further investigation?

4. Compare articles of your choice in the *International Standard*

Bible Encyclopedia (1915/1929) edited by James Orr, and the revised *International Standard Bible Encyclopedia* (1979-88) edited by G. W. Bromiley. How do these articles compare biblically, theologically, and scholastically?

5. Take special note of the indices at the end of the encyclopedias and dictionaries listed above. How varied and comprehensive are they? Are Greek and Hebrew word studies included?

2

General Reference Works
Part 1

RELIGIOUS AND BIBLICAL

Sitting in a church history class at the beginning of a new semester, Brett Bartlett listened halfheartedly as the professor droned on about the course. The professor's approach projected the attitude that church history was dull, and in the opinion of upper classmen he taught each of his courses as if it were his duty to perpetuate that impression. Brett vaguely remembers hearing:

"Each of you will be required to prepare a documented research paper on a topic which I will assign. It will be due the first class period following the Thanksgiving recess. I will now go down the class roll and assign each of you your topic.

"Adams. I want you to write on 'Abjuration'

"Anderson. Your topic is 'Adoptionism.'

"Aske. Your assignment is the 'Rise of the Bishopric.'

"Bartlett, you are to write on the 'Cluniacs.'"

Later Brett came to the reference desk. "Who are the 'Kluniaks'" he asked. He had scrawled the name on a piece of paper and we noticed at once that it was spelled incorrectly. "I've checked the catalog and can't find a single reference to them!"

We sensed his frustration. As we began the search for data, we consulted the index volume of James Hastings' *Encyclopedia of Religion and Ethics*. There we were referred to a lengthy article on "Monasticism" with an entire section devoted to the founding of the Cluniacs. This article, together with other resources located through the bibliography, took only a few minutes to locate, and the seemingly "Himalayan" task Brett had faced had been reduced to size.

We share this story out of the belief that a knowledge of bibliographic research (i.e., research methodology that begins with general reference works) can completely revolutionize a student's outlook toward his or her studies. From college freshmen to seniors, and even those in graduate school, many who once dreaded using the library suddenly loose their fear of not being able to find what they are looking for as soon as they master the use of certain basic resources. After this they find that research can be fun. Furthermore, as their outlook changes and success crowns their efforts, their grades improve. And the secret? *They have learned how to work smarter, not just harder.*

As mentioned in our previous chapter, one proven way of researching a topic is to *begin* with general reference works and then move to specific resources. This is invariably done by referring to encyclopedias and dictionaries to see what information they contain on the topic you have either chosen or had assigned to you. While these resources are most often arranged in "dictionary format" (i.e., the topics are listed in alphabetical order [e.g., from "Aaron" to "Zuzim"]), it is always wise to consult the index (if the resource tool you are using has one).

It is not our purpose or desire to slight or ignore the general encyclopedias like the *New Encyclopedia Britannica* or the *Encyclopedia Americana*, or to talk about *Encyclopedia Britannica Online* (accessible through the Internet) and the *Encarta* (on CD-ROM), and the other fine general encyclopedias. Our discussion will be devoted chiefly (but not exclusively) to some of the more scholarly works that are of a biblical and theological nature.

By definition, an encyclopedia is usually a multi-volume work that contains a collection of articles giving essential information about the various branches of knowledge. Its arrangement is almost always alphabetically by subject. Specialized (or subject) encyclopedias (e.g., devoted to archaeology, or the Bible, or ethics, or philosophy) contain articles bearing on a specific field of knowledge or area of interest.

As a general principle, a student should use an encyclopedia when he or she first begins to probe the parameters of a topic, or desires to refresh his or her memory on certain specifics, or wants to ascertain who the leaders were (or are) who contributed to the growth of knowledge in a particular area. One semester we found that undergraduates were all writing term papers on "leadership." And, of course, the young women wanted to write articles on "Women in Leadership." They came to us to find out what information might be stored on the Internet. None of them thought to consult an encyclopedia to find out about the different kinds of leaders and the strengths and weaknesses of their styles. We feared that their papers might end up being little more that a summary of a journal article they had chosen.

Encyclopedias, of course, have been prepared for different audiences: e.g., children or youth, college and/or graduate students, professional researchers (e.g., chemists, scientists, engineers), academicians and/or learned individuals, and subject specialists (e.g., oceanographers, climatologists, seismologists)—to name a few. Our focus will be on the more scholarly works. In this connection we are unashamedly biased. While appreciating the contribution of modern research, we do not want to ignore the rich heritage of the past. Truth is timeless, and though information in other disciplines may quickly become dated, truth in theology and related fields of inquiry retains its value.

Each encyclopedia has its strengths and weaknesses. For example, Patrick Fairbairn's *Imperial Standard Bible Encyclopedia* (6 vols.; 1889/ 1957) is particularly good when treating Bible characters. It would be excellent for researching material on Balaam, Deborah, Elihu, Fortunatus, Gershom, Hiram, Ittai, Jabez, and a host of others. On the other hand, the *Encyclopedia Biblica* (4 vols.; 1899-1903) by T. K. Cheyne and J. S. Black, is a scholarly work evidencing a high degree of accuracy and completeness, but it is marred by the adherence of the contributors to negative theories about the Bible.

The question naturally arises, How can someone who is not a subject specialist (i.e., untrained in Biblical studies, church music, historical and systematic theology, the original languages, etc.) discern which encyclopedias or dictionaries of religion are worthy of the investment of one's time (and perhaps money), and which are not? The answer to this question can be outlined as follows:

- Is the encyclopedia or dictionary authoritative? Is the editor a person of repute? Have the articles been signed (the assumption being that if a person's name concludes the article, he or she will have taken extra special care in writing it)? Are the contributors people of established reputation?

- Why was this work written (i.e., what need did the editor seek to be meet), and for whom? (This information is generally found in the Introduction or Preface.)

- What is its scope? (i.e., is the coverage comprehensive?) Are the articles long or short? Is the thrust biblical or theological, denominational (e.g., Roman Catholic, Mennonite, Reformed, etc.), interfaith, national or international?

- How up to date is it? Is it an entirely new work, or has it been based on an earlier edition with the same or a different title? How reliable are the maps, charts, money conversions, et cetera?

- What are the recognizable strong points? What features make this work superior to any others? Does it have any weaknesses or acknowledged limitations?

In using an encyclopedia or dictionary, you will want to know something about its contents, organization, arrangement (alphabetically letter-by-letter or alphabetically word-by-word), indexes and general usefulness. We plan to discuss encyclopedias of religion before considering those dealing specifically with the Bible. Our approach will illustrate some of these points. The scope of an encyclopedia of religion is obviously broader than an encyclopedia that is limited solely to the Bible.

Encyclopedias of Religion

In this category we will focus our attention on the following:

Encyclopedia of Religion and Ethics, ed. J. Hastings.

Cyclopedia of Biblical, Theological, and Ecclesiastical Literature, eds. J. M'Clintock and J. Strong.

New Catholic Encyclopedia.

New Schaff-Herzog Encyclopedia of Religious Knowledge, ed. S. M. Jackson.

Encyclopedia Judaica.

Encyclopedia of Religion, ed. M. Eliade.

Encyclopedia of American Religious Experience, ed. C. H. Lippy and P. W. Williams.

Encyclopedia of American Religious History, ed. J. G. Melton.

And we will conclude this section by mentioning very briefly two works—the one treating New Age beliefs, and the other cults, sects, and the occult.

The *Encyclopedia of Religion and Ethics* (often cited as *HERE*), edited by James Hastings (12 vols., plus index; 1908-27), is a comprehensive work with long, scholarly, signed articles dealing with "all the religions of the world and all the great systems of ethics," together with a wide variety of theological and philosophical topics. It includes a discussion of religious beliefs and customs, and moral practices. Also to be found within these volumes is data on anthropology, folklore, mythology, biology, psychology, economics, and sociology—and the people and places connected with a variety of diverse events or practices. Extensive, though now dated, bibliographies conclude most articles. A comprehensive index, together with a list of article titles and an exhaustive subject index conclude this important work.

In keeping with all the multi-volume works edited by James Hastings, *HERE* contains numerous "See" references interspersed throughout the major articles. The contributors were all scholars who in their day were considered specialists in their respective fields. Each article gives evidence of being well researched and the product of mature reflection. In fact, after consulting articles on topics like "Love," "Magi," "Marriage," "Mary," "Meekness," "Mercy," "Messiah," "Messiah (Pseudo)," "Mind," et cetera, it is not surprising that more recent works have relatively little new material to contribute.

Although dated in matters of history and archaeology, and lacking information on some of the newer religious movements, *HERE* is still worth consulting. "Abortion" receives extensive treatment under "Feticide," and a discussion of "homosexuality" is to be found under "Sodomy." The subject index contains a valuable listing of topics which may well spark your interest when you are required to write a paper on a "subject of your choice" and do not know where to begin.

Of a similar nature is the *Cyclopedia of Biblical, Theological, and Ecclesiastical Literature*, edited by James M'Clintock and James Strong (10 vols.; 1867-1881. Supplement, 1894. Reprinted 1968-1970). This *Cyclopedia* is by far the most comprehensive and rewarding work available today. It comprises articles commissioned and collected by two American scholars who ranked among the most learned people of their day. The articles are generally long and give evidence of being well researched. They cover all of Christendom and many of the non-Christian religions. Coverage of topics such as Pelagianism, antinomianism, and scholasticism are of such significance that you will rarely find that the time spent consulting this work has been wasted. And information on notable persons of the Bible around whose lives so much is built in both the Old and the New Testaments (e.g., Adam and Eve, Abraham, Moses, David, the Apostles, and Paul) exhibit a thoroughness that is truly satisfying.

When writing the Introduction to the 1968-1970 reprint, Wilbur M. Smith said: "Even though a century has passed since the first volume was published, many articles in these pages are still superior to, and more comprehensive than, articles on the same subjects appearing in any other similar work."

This set is particularly strong in areas of biography (e.g., "Anselm," "Calvin," "Erasmus," "Stephen Langdon," "Menno Simons," and many more), biblical geography, critical issues, customs and cultures, denominations and their growth, and a variety of other themes. "See" references are used in appropriate places and representative bibliographies conclude many of the longer essays. And articles on topics like "Abomination," "Antichrist," "Bible," "Confession," "Crucifixion," "Infallibility," "Messianic Hope," "Millennium," "Pelagianism." "Ring," "Sabbath," "Sacrament," "Samuel," "Sin," et cetera, are all extremely well done.

The set was updated in 1894 with two supplemental volumes of approximately 1000 pages each. These have been included in the 1968-1970 reprint.

The *New Catholic Encyclopedia*, prepared by the editorial staff of the Catholic University of America, Washington, D.C. (15 vols. plus index; 1967; Supplement 1967-1974; Supplement 1975-1979), is, in spite of its title, entirely new and bears no relation to the earlier *Catholic Encyclopedia* (17 vols.; 1907-22). Researchers who consult both works will find that this one reflects the more tolerant views and policies of the post-Vatican II era.

Arranged alphabetically, the articles reflect maturity as well as reliability, and while manifesting a tendency to devote more space to the Catholic church in the United States and Latin America than to Catholicism in other parts of the world, they cover virtually every aspect of Catholic history, theology and ministry. Each of the 17,000 articles is signed, and helpful bibliographies are appended to many of them.

Among the plethora of articles of interest to Protestants are the following: Pagan religious rites (e.g., associated with the worship of Baal and the Asherah); biographical sketches of modern scholars (e.g., Martin Dibelius, Rudolf Otto); informative studies of cities now famous as a result of recent archaeological excavations (Mari, Nuzi, Ugarit); people of note in the history of the church (e.g., Gregory the Great [however, Victor of St. Hugo and some other important evangelical leaders have been omitted]); champions of biblical exegesis (e.g., J. B. Lightfoot, B. F. Westcott); prominent missiologists (e.g., William Carey, Albert Schweitzer); American educators and theologians (e.g., Timothy Dwight, Jonathan Edwards, B. B. Warfield); and, of course, numerous articles on philosophers and their systems of thought.

While some authorities (according to the dust cover) regard the *New Schaff-Herzog Encyclopedia of Religious Knowledge*, edited by S. M. Jackson (12 vols. and index; 1908-1912/1969) as the "best known," "most authoritative" and "most widely used" of Protestant encyclopedias, the strength of this set lies in the familiarity of the contributors with German theology, European church history, and philosophical trends on the Continent up to and including the turn of the century. Often cited as *SHERK*, its appeal is more for those holding to a liturgical tradition.

SHERK is based upon the third edition of the Herzog-Hauk *Realencyklopadie*. The articles that comprise the English translation and expansion of the German original deal cogently and yet concisely with Protestant theology, church history, missions, philosophy, sects and isms, and much more. The articles are all signed and have been contributed by respected scholars. Biographical sketches of people who may otherwise be difficult to research (e.g., John Eadie, John Kitto, William Cunningham) constitute a valuable addition. In some instances, however, the bibliographic sources cited are erroneous. Nevertheless, what is presented is worthy of consideration. Readers are well advised to consult volume 13 (index) of *SHERK* when doing research.

Approximately forty years after the appearance of this English edition, two supplementary volumes entitled *Twentieth Century Encyclopedia of Religious Knowledge*, edited by Lefferts A. Loetscher (1950-1955), were added. These supplements contain alphabetically arranged articles updating the original work. These articles, however, have not been included in the index to the set.

The modern *Encyclopedia Judaica,* edited by C. Roth et al (16 vols.; 1972) was produced after the establishment of the State of Israel in 1948. It has now replaced the earlier *Jewish Encyclopedia*, edited by Isidore Singer et al (12 vols.; 1901-1906), and the *Universal Jewish Encyclopedia*, edited by Isaac Landman et al (11 vols.; 1939-1944).

Before discussing *EJ*, however, a few words need to be said about the abiding usefulness of the *Universal Jewish Encyclopedia*. *UJE* is replete with information about the "Jews and Judaism since the earliest times." It consists of a compilation of 10,000 lengthy, signed articles on Jewish history, religion, and culture and customs, and it is ideal for Bible character studies (e.g., "Aaron," "Barak," "David," "Elijah," "Gehazi," "Moses," "Jonah," etc.) as well as the Jewish feasts (e.g., Trumpets, Purim) and fasts (Yom Kippur).

While following an alphabetical sequence, the major articles are classified under seven headings: History (treating, among other topics, the era of the Patriarchs; the construction and significance to Israel of the Tabernacle and its furnishings; the priesthood and its functions; David; the kingdom; and races (such as Syrians, Assyrians, Neo-Babylonians, and Persians, etc.); *Literature* (including the development and relationship of the different Semitic languages, *hapax legomena*, Hebrew lexicography, an analysis of Hebrew prose, poetry and wisdom literature, the rise of the apocryphal and pseudepigraphal writings, and allegorical interpretation, etc.); *Religion* (dealing with the rise of monotheism, a delineation of the various pagan deities encountered in the Old Testament, an assessment of Hebrew doctrine described as "Articles of Faith," ethical and social standards, spirituality, the names of God, the nature of man, and a discussion of customs and ceremonies); *Jewish Life* (including the family, the education of children, the place of the synagogue, and different legal procedures); the relationship of *Jews and Non-Jews* (describing the attitude of Jews toward other religions, including Christianity; their view of Christian doctrine; Gentile writers who have written on Jewish themes; anti-Semitism); *General* (archaeology and the Bible, folklore, symbolism, Messianic movements, the Messianic era, democracy, proselytes, etc.); and *Jewish Contributions to Civilization* (in and through art, architecture, the humanities, the sciences, etc.).

While *UJE* is one which Protestants can use with profit, it has now been superseded by the more recent *Encyclopedia Judaica*. Biblical information in *EJ* is not as full or as complete as in *UJE*, but it does contain information on the latest archaeological findings as well as the history of Judaism. It is well indexed and has extensive cross-references. Hebrew words are transliterated, and bibliographies contain references to important, recent monographs.

EJ offers a comprehensive and up-to-date view of Judaism. The 25,000 articles have been written by men and women of international repute. Most of the articles have been initialed by the author. All but the briefest entries contain bibliographies. Living persons are included among the biographies. Supplements were planned to cover new material, but only issued through to the end of 1981. Yearbooks (1973-) vary in frequency.

The Encyclopedia of Religion, edited by M. Eliade et al (16 vols.; 1987) took seven years to complete. It contains 2,750 signed articles and comprises about 8,000 pages. The contributors are all capable scholars. It is to be regretted, however, that few of them are evangelical and none are truly conservative in their theology. The articles are arranged in alphabetic order, but the use of the Index volume is encouraged. No distinction is made between revelatory religion and those of purely human origin. All are treated as the product of a founder (e.g., Buddha, Mohammed, Moses, Jesus, Paul, etc.). Useful bibliographies conclude each article.

Each religion is presented with its "important ideas, beliefs, rituals, myths, symbols and persons that played a role in the universal history of religions from Paleolithic times to the present day." The treatment of biblical topics will mislead the uninformed student. For example, the chronology of the Israelite settlement in Canaan is faulty, as is the early history of the Philistines, Aramaeans, and Arabs. Other errors permeate the discussions of biblical topics.

Articles treating non-revelatory religions, as well as biographies of leading individuals, have generally been well done. The important doctrines as well as key happenings alert the reader to different crises or explain to the reader the historic "hinges" on which significant events took place. All things considered, this is a useful encyclopedia and should prove helpful to the student of comparative religions.

Encyclopedia of American Religious Experience, edited by C. H. Lippy and P. W. Williams, (3 vols.; 1988) consists of 105 long, interpretative essays by authorities in the fields of history, religion, American studies, sociology, and philosophy. The articles are arranged logically and topically within nine broad categories. Prominence is given "liturgy, worship, and the arts." A select bibliography and cross-references have been appended to each essay. An extensive index provides the student with quick access to a plethora of topics discussed in a variety of different articles. There is also an alphabetical list of articles and a list of contributors. The comprehensiveness of this encyclopedia is commendable.

The Encyclopedia of American Religions (4th ed.; 1993), by J. G. Melton is an authoritative source of information on American religious groups, both large and small. The introductory essays are particularly apropos. They document religious history in the U.S. and Canada, and then discuss "religious families" (e.g., Catholic, Protestant, Jewish, etc.). Included is a directory providing historical and contemporary information. The work is well indexed.

Two other books of related interest are G. A. Mather and L. A. Nichols' *Dictionary of Cults, Sects, Religions and the Occult* (1993), and J. Ankerberg and J. Weldon's *Encyclopedia of New Age Beliefs* (1996). The former is arranged in dictionary format (i.e., containing articles from "A.'A.'" and Mormonism's "Aaronic Priesthood" to "Zul Hijiah" and "Zwinglianism"). The material is pertinent to the present times and readily answers the kinds of questions regularly asked of pastors. The latter work is more narrowly focused, even though it does overlap in part the *Dictionary* of Mather and Nichols. *ENAB* provides essays (some of which cover several pages) on such topics as "Altered States of Consciousness," "Channeling," "Mantras and Mandalas," "New Age Education," "Scientology," and "Visualization" (to name only a few). This is an excellent work, and we are grateful for its availability.

Encyclopedias and Dictionaries of the Bible

Having considered some of the strengths and weaknesses of encyclopedias of religion, we can now narrow our focus and consider some of the more useful biblical works. In this category we will evaluate:

Anchor Bible Dictionary, ed. D. N. Freedman et al.

New Unger's Bible Dictionary, ed. R. K. Harrison

Dictionary of the Bible (5 vol. ed.), ed. J. Hastings

Dictionary of Jesus and the Gospels, eds. J. B. Green, S. McKnight, and I. H. Marshall

Dictionary of Paul and His Letters, eds. G. F. Hawthorne, R. P. Martin, and D. G. Reid

Dictionary of the Later New Testament and Its Developments, eds. R. P. Martin and P. H. Davids

Dictionary of Biblical Imagery, eds. L. Ryken, J. C. Wilhoit, and T. Longman III

Interpreter's Dictionary of the Bible, ed. G. A. Buttrick

International Standard Bible Encyclopedia, ed. J. Orr, 1915/1929; revised edition ed. G. W. Bromiley, 1979-1988

Zondervan Pictorial Encyclopedia of the Bible, ed. M. C. Tenney.

The Anchor Bible Dictionary, edited by D. N. Freedman et al (6 vols.; 1992), is the product of nearly 1,000 scholars from all parts of the world. There are approximately 6,200 entries with some of them extending to 40 pages. They cover proper names, major words, the different books of the Bible (together with comments on the relevance of the Apocryphal texts, the Dead Sea Scrolls, and the Nag Hammadi codices). All the articles are signed and the longer ones have bibliographies appended to them that range in length from a few entries to three or more columns. The emphasis is slanted toward archaeological evidence. The contributors are decidedly non-conservative in their handling of the biblical text. However, there is something of value in each article. Hebrew and Greek words are transliterated for the sake of those who do not have a knowledge of the original languages.

Some idea of the coverage given different archaeological sites can be gauged by comparing information on "Beitin, Tell" and "Bethel." Written by two different scholars they treat the history and problems of identification of the city from two separate perspectives. In some articles distances are given in miles and in others in kilometers. The dating of certain Old Testament events nearly always follows the late (and more liberal) school of thought.

Examples of good articles are: "Child, Children," "Covenant," "Levites and Priests," "Marriage (Old Testament and Ancient Near East)," "Stoics, Stoicism," and "Weapons and Implements of Warfare." There are two articles on "Mesopotamia, History of" (with the first treating

Assyria and the second Babylonia). Less reliable entries deal with such issues as the "Synoptic Problem," "Textual Criticism," and different Christological/theological themes. This dictionary is now available on CD-ROM.

Though much briefer, the *New Unger's Bible Dictionary* edited by R. K. Harrison (1988), is more reliable. It is based on the *Bible Encyclopedia* by C. R. Barnes (1900), and was thoroughly revised and updated by Merrill F. Unger in 1957. Unger revised it again in 1961. It is probably the most helpful one-volume Bible dictionary available today, having now been brought up to date by R. K. Harrison. The entire work is marked by consistency. Archaeological information is reliable. The history and chronology of biblical events are accurate. Descriptions of places, as well as the manners and customs of people living in Bible times (c2000 B.C. to A.D. 100) are most helpful. Representative bibliographies conclude most important articles.

Dictionary of the Bible, edited by James Hastings (5 vols.; 1898-1904), is designed for those "entrusted with the responsibility of teaching the Word of God." This impressive work is the result of predominately British scholarship. Each article is signed, and many of the longer ones have important bibliographies appended to them. "See" references are used in the body of some of the essays and at the end of others.

Although more moderate in its stance than *Encyclopedia Biblica* by Cheyne and Black, readers will still find that many higher critical theories are espoused by the contributors. In spite of that weakness, HDB contains informative articles on all persons and places, ethnology and geology, natural history and biblical theology, and even deals with archaic words occurring in different English versions of the Bible.

Volume five contains thirty-seven extensive additional articles covering topics like the "Sermon on the Mount," "New Testament Times," the "Talmud," "Races of the Old Testament," "The Religion of Israel," et cetera. These are not arranged in alphabetical order. Invaluable indices to all articles, authors, Scripture texts, Hebrew and Greek terms, illustrations, and maps provide ready access to the wealth of material to be found in the dictionary.

Because recent archaeological finds have illuminated much of Bible history, geography, customs, and culture, a work of this nature obviously has its deficiencies. However, on those occasions when you wish to consult an article on a topic like "Roads and Travel," "Style of Scripture," "The Trinity," or "Versions of the Bible," you immediately become impressed with the wealth of scholarship evidenced in each article. For this reason, HDB is still worth consulting.

A one-volume abridgment was issued in 1909. In 1963 it was reissued, having been revised and updated by F. C. Grant and H. H. Rowley. Certain new entries treating new items like the Dead Sea Scrolls and some biblical terms omitted from the earlier edition were included.

The Dictionary of Jesus and the Gospels, edited by J. B. Green, S. McKnight, and I. H. Marshall (1992) is an attempt on the part of the editors to provide a replacement for the *Dictionary of Christ and the Gospels,* edited by James Hastings (2 vols.; 1906-1908. Reissued as volumes 1 and 2 under the title *Dictionary of the New Testament, [4* vols.; 1973]).

Before discussing the newer *Dictionary of Jesus and the Gospels,* we need to know something about the work it is supposed to be replacing.

Hastings' *Dictionary of Christ and the Gospels* (abbreviated *HDCG*) follows a similar format to *HDB.* Like *HDB* it is primarily the product of British scholarship, and is designed to focus attention specifically on the person, work and teaching of Christ. In this respect it is complementary to *HDB,* with the editor's stated purpose being "mainly with things biographical, historical, geographical, or antiquarian."

Excellent, lengthy, signed articles highlight the places of Christ's ministry, the traditions and practices of the Jews, and the preaching style of the Lord Jesus. Also included are expressions like "Only Begotten," and "the Brethren of Our Lord" that appear in the biblical record. In all, 2,000 topics have been covered. Of particular value are the biographical sketches--of people encountered for the first time the Gospel records, and also of Old Testament personalities referred to by Christ (e.g., "Noah," "Balaam," "Moses," "Jonah," "Joshua," "Queen of Sheba,"). *HDCG* is replete with indexes of subjects, Greek terms and Scripture texts. This set will handsomely repay the researcher for his or her efforts.

While manifesting the same "left wing" theological tendencies as *HDB,* these volumes have achieved deserved praise from Bible scholars and may be consulted with profit.

The Dictionary of Jesus and the Gospels was designed to provide in a handy, accessible, single volume format data explaining the things that the Lord Jesus said and did. It contains approximately 200 lengthy, signed articles that cover the four gospels, and it discusses just about every related topic about which one might seek information. Representative bibliographies conclude each article.

Such a work is needed. The editors, however, tip their hand when they describe *DJG* as a "work of Protestant scholarship that attempts to be both critically responsible and theologically evangelical." This rhetoric is merely a cover for the fact that most of the biblical and theological articles in *DJG* are based upon *Redaktionsgeschichte* (i.e., redaction criticism). *DJG* would be better described as a neoevangelical approach to the life of Christ with occasional neo-orthodox ideas thrown in. When compared with *HDCG*, that is avowedly liberal, this work requires greater care and attention on the part of the user, for its biases are subtler.

A companion volume to *DJG* is the *Dictionary of Paul and His Letters*, edited by G. F. Hawthorne, R. P. Martin, and D. G. Reid (1993). According to the publishers, it is intended to replace (at least in part) James Hastings' *Dictionary of the Apostolic Church*. Once again it is incumbent upon us to know something about the earlier work before we discard it as obsolete. Hastings' *Dictionary of the Apostolic Church* (2 vols.; 1915. Reissued as volumes 3 and 4 of the *Dictionary of the New Testament*, 1973), supplements *HDB* and *HDAC*, and carries the history of Christianity through the period covered by the Book of Acts to the close of the first century. While there is a greater representation of articles by American scholars in *DAC* than in either *HDB* or *HDAC*, British contributors still predominate.

A careful perusal of *DAC* yields the fact that adequate attention is given extra-biblical source materials (e.g., the Apocryphal writings) as well as less obvious topics like human emotions ("Anger," "Jealousy," "Love"). Biographical articles are again prominent, and these vary in length from a few lines to several pages. Doctrinal issues likewise receive extensive treatment and are frequently linked with the teaching of the Old Testament (e.g., "Atonement").

Each book of the New Testament (the Gospels excepted) is carefully outlined, introduced and commented on in such a way as to bring out its primary purpose and message. Perhaps the greatest single asset of this set is the manner in which historic events are used to highlight biblical teachings (e.g. "Adoption," "Emperor worship," the development of the law, etc.). In addition, the correlation of historical references with people and places, cities and events (e.g., "Paul and Tarsus," "John and Patmos," and the cities referred to in Revelation chs. 2--3) all add such richness to the study of different New Testament passages that the reader is left enthralled by what he or she has learned.

While these volumes do not match the brilliance of those dealing with Christ and the Gospels, they should be consulted whenever one is studying the expansion of the early church.

Turning now to the *Dictionary of Paul and His Letters*, we find it to be a masterpiece of condensed information. Most of the lengthy articles include both a diachronic treatment of his letters and a synchronic treatment of their contents according to the major topic. A few of the tables are of extraordinary help. While claiming to be evangelical, many of the contributors can best be described as neoevangelical. As in the companion volume cited above, *DPL* contains signed articles with scholarly bibliographies. However, like *DJG*, most of the articles are built upon critical theories about the composition of these letters, and this seriously reduces the value of *DPL* for the Bible student and busy pastor. Even though this work has much to commend it, the same concerns mention in relation to *DJG* apply here.

The *Dictionary of the Later New Testament and Its Developments* comments on everything from "Abba" to "Wrath, Destruction." It contains over 230 lengthy articles, and its usefulness is enhanced by numerous cross-references, extensive bibliographies, and subject and Scripture indexes. It provides a clear, theological analysis of each of the NT books not covered in previous volumes (e.g., "Acts"), and is replete with character studies (e.g., "Abraham") as well as the historical development of Christianity (e.g., "Alexandria, Alexandrian Christianity"), as well as special topics (e.g., "Ancestors," "Antichrist"). Each article is signed and helpful bibliographies conclude each major discussion. The overall tone is neoevangelical. Will meet the felt need of seminarians.

The *Dictionary of Biblical Imagery* serves as an excellent introduction to the literature of the Bible, its archetypes, plot motifs, rhetorical devices, literary genres, and the themes of the different books of the Bible. Of particular value is the way in which the 160 contributors explore the fascinating and varied world of biblical imagery (including a discussion of the different metaphors and other figures of speech). It includes articles on subjects like "Beatitude," "Birthright," "Black," "Blindness," "Body," "Bread," "Bride, Bridegroom", "Brimstone," "Burning Bush" and much more. The longer articles contain numerous cross-references. Replete with bibliographies.

The *Interpreter's Dictionary of the Bible*, edited by G. A. Buttrick et al (4 vols.; 1962), is similar in range, scope and purpose to Hastings's *Dictionary of the Bible*. *IDB* however, aims at providing identifications and explanations of "all proper names, significant terms, and subjects in the Holy Scriptures, including the Apocrypha." Signed articles contributed by recognized authorities (most of them from the United States), and brief, up-to-date bibliographies for further study, make this work a model of modern scholarship. Numerous cross references enhance this resource. The user soon becomes aware of the fact that nearly all of the contributors build upon negative biblical criticism. This necessitates that care be taken lest the unwary be swept along by plausible interpretations of the biblical text that appear reasonable on the surface only to be found to undermine the authority of the Scriptures. Experience has shown that this process inevitably looses credibility as later scholarship exposes the inherent weaknesses of such an approach.

In contrast to the other works cited in this chapter, *IDB* contains factual data about fairly recent archaeological finds and, in some places, incorporates this information into the discussion of the biblical text. For the most part, however, this information is included as the development of a particular subject dictates, but without attempting to show how it confirms or elucidates the teaching of Scripture.

IDB is also valuable for the pronunciation given different words at the beginning of some articles, the etymology of Hebrew, Aramaic or Greek words, and an explanation of their meanings. The text upon which this work is based is the Revised Standard Version of the Bible (RSV). Most of the entries are short and vary in length from one paragraph to one page. Some articles, however, are much longer and may run up to thirty pages or more (cf., "Versions of Scripture," "Jesus Christ," etc.). A supplementary volume, edited by Keith Crum, was published in 1976. While this set received acclaim as "excellent" for those "beginning research on a biblical subject," the theological orientation of many of the contributors necessitates that *IDB* be used with discernment.

The *International Standard Bible Encyclopedia*, edited by J. Orr et al (5 vols.; 1915; rev. ed. 1929), is described by the editors as advocating a "reasonable conservatism." From the very first *ISBE* was intended to provide a reliable guide to the history of peoples and religions encountered in both the Old and New Testaments as well as the ethnology, geography, topography, biography, arts and crafts, manners and customs, family life, natural history, agriculture, war, commerce, ritual, laws, sects, music, "and all else pertaining to the outer and inner life of the people of the Bible."

To accomplish this task, a team of international scholars was assembled, over one hundred of whom were from the United States, about sixty from Great Britain and Europe, and the rest from other parts of the world. The result was an interdenominational work that soon achieved a deserved place on the bookshelf of pastors and teachers of all persuasions.

While this edition of *ISBE* now shares the same limitations as *HDB* and other older encyclopedias, it nevertheless contains articles by some of the greatest scholars of Christendom, and this gives it a certain timeless quality. These contributors include men of the caliber of W. F. Albright, T. Witton Davies, J. Garstang, A. S. Geden, M. G. Kyle, T. M. Lindsay, H. C. G. Moule, W. M. Flinders Petrie, A. T. Robertson, H. Strack, W. H. Griffith Thomas, and B. B. Warfield, to name only a few.

The articles are signed, and the longer ones contain "See" references and a bibliography listing books and articles representing all viewpoints. Volume 5 contains a "List of Contributors," a general index, index of Scripture texts, and two other valuable indices: (1) to Hebrew and Aramaic words; and (2) to Greek words.

Beginning in 1979 and finishing in 1988, Wm. B. Eerdmans Publishing Company issued a revision of *ISBE* in four volumes. The new project was under the general editorship of Geoffrey W. Bromiley. A list of the contributors appears in volume 1, and readers are alerted to those contributors whose article(s) from the first edition have been retained. While less conservative than the former edition, this new *ISBE* meets a real need, particularly in areas where former encyclopedias no longer are able to supply up-to-date information.

The *Zondervan Pictorial Encyclopedia of the Bible*, edited by M. C. Tenney et al (5 vols.; 1975), enlarges upon the one-volume *Zondervan Pictorial Bible Dictionary* (1963) and is, in general, the product of conservative theological scholarship. The list of contributors in the front of volume 1 gives evidence of the international and interdenominational scope of this important reference tool.

The articles vary in length from a few lines to book-length treatises (e.g., "Jesus Christ," "Paul"). All the articles are signed; "See" references have been used to good effect, and the bibliographies reflect a wide range of literature. As is indicated by the title, this work is enhanced by the inclusion of numerous photographs, maps and drawings.

Where necessary, articles begin with the correct pronunciation of the word or name, followed by the Hebrew and/or Greek form together with an explanation of the etymology. Each essay is well outlined, clear and concise. Biblical references are numerous. Contributions like "Archaeology," "Biblical Theology," "Canon," "Education in Bible Times," "Herod," "Inspiration," "Interpretation," "Jerusalem," a correlation of the history and chronology of Egypt with that of Israel, and character studies of familiar and unfamiliar persons encountered on the pages of God's Word, place at the fingertips of the researcher a wide variety of factual material. Other items worth noting are the defense of the integrity of Paul's Ephesian letter and able treatments of topics like "Eternity," "Exile," "Eye salve," and much more. There is no subject index or foreign word index. All things considered, this work deserves to be consulted whenever you are researching biblical topics.

LOOKING AHEAD

1. Familiarize yourself with M. Avi-Yonah and E. Stein's *New Encyclopedia of Archaeological Excavations in the Holy Land.* As

you consider the life of Abraham (particularly as recorded in Genesis 12), to what extent is light shed on the life and times of the patriarch (i.e., by providing information on some of the cities he lived in or passed by), the route he followed from Ur in southern Mesopotamia to Hebron (e.g., Shechem, Bethel, Beersheba) and even the customs and culture of the people he encountered?

2. Greek words and their meanings are handled in Colin Brown's *New International Dictionary of New Testament Theology* (3 vols. plus index), and G. Kittel and G. Friedrich's *Theological Dictionary of the New Testament* (9 vols. plus index). Assess the scope of each work by considering the way in which respective writers have handled words like "Heal," and its cognates; "Heart," "King, Kingdom."

3. Compare the articles on "Kingdom," "Man," and "Pardon" in W. A. Elwell's *Evangelical Dictionary of Theology*, and A. Richardson's *Dictionary of Christian Theology*. What is the theological perspective of each writer? Is the article written from a biblical, historical, philosophical, or theological point of view? From which secondary sources does the writer draw his information? On a scale of one-to-ten (with ten being best), how would you rate each article for (a) general usefulness, (b) reliability, and (c) coverage of important issues?

3

General Reference Works
Part 2

BIBLICAL ARCHAEOLOGY AND THEOLOGY

Biblical Archaeology Reference Works

Archaeology adds unique interest to our study of the Bible. On numerous occasions it confirms the historical accuracy of what is taught in God's Word, while at other times it illustrates important doctrines of our faith. And then there are those occasions when it clarifies different idioms or customs.

Let us illustrate what we mean. Every year thousands of tourists visit Athens. Some of them are satisfied with a bus tour of the city and a stop at the famous Acropolis to stretch their legs as they walk around the Parthenon. Then they're off to the airport to spend a couple of days in Rome or Zurich, Luxembourg or Vienna. They may see a lot, but they learn very little.

One never-to-be-forgotten Greek excursion is a visit to the ancient site of Delphi, northwest of Athens, near Mount Parnassos. There, in the ruins of the temple of Apollo, are to be found some inscriptions that shed light on the Apostle Paul's teaching of redemption. One of these inscriptions tells of a girl named Nicaea, who was *ransomed* from slavery—bought from a man named Sosibius—for the specific purpose of being set free (cf. 1 Corinthians 6:20; 7:23. See also Galatians 4:5). This touching human-interest story from remote antiquity graphically portrays what the Lord Jesus did for all who place their trust in Him. Once released from their enslavement to sin, He sets us free (cf. 1 Corinthians 7:22-23, 35).[5]

Archaeology also confirms the fact that human nature hasn't changed in thousands of years. A man, who lived in ancient Mesopotamia, in the city of Assur, borrowed some money for a business venture. He then left Assur, and it took a long time for his creditors to locate him. When they did, this is what they wrote:

> Thirty years ago you left the city of Assur. You have never made a deposit (i.e., of interest on the loan), and we have not recovered one shekel of silver from you. But we have never made you feel bad about this. Our tablets have been going to you with caravan after caravan, but no report (i.e., response) from you has ever come here.... Should you be too busy with your business, deposit the silver for us....
>
> If not, we will send you a notice from the local ruler and the police, and thus put you to shame in the assembly of the merchants. You will also cease to be one of us.[6]

As it was then, so it is now. People defraud one another and hope that they will never be called to account for their actions (Numbers 32:32). Even when sin catches up with them, God deals graciously with them, giving them time to repent. If they do not, then He has ways and means whereby their sin is exposed thus bringing shame upon them.

But what of the idioms or customs mentioned in the Bible? Does archaeology shed light on these, too? One of our goals as students of God's Word should be accuracy in interpretation, and a knowledge of archaeology sheds light on the Bible's usage of words or the practice of its people. Consider, for example, how archaeological data illumines Judas' "sale" of the Lord Jesus to the chief priests. Scripture records that all he asked for was thirty pieces of silver (Matthew 26:15). This has puzzled Bible students for ages. The question, put very simply, is "Why did Judas sell Christ for so little?"

For the longest time all Bible teachers could do was point to Exodus 21:32 and tell us that this was the compensation paid to an owner when his slave had been gored to death by an ox. But Judas did not "own" Christ, nor was the Lord his slave. And the Lord Jesus had not been killed at the time the money was paid to him. How then are we to understand the significance of this reference?

Information has come to us from Sumerian archives suggesting that thirty pieces of silver was a term of contempt. When the king of Agade went to conquer other kingdoms and enrich himself from the spoils of war, he came eventually to Nippur. He deemed it to be too poor—not "worth thirty shekels of silver"—to be worthy of conquest.

Confirmation of this use of "thirty shekels of silver" as an expression implying something of trifling significance is to be found in the "Epic of Gilgamesh." This poem recounts the exploits of the mythical hero, Gilgamesh. One line tells how, when Gilgamesh put on his armor (weighing fifty minas), it seemed to him as if it weighed no more then thirty shekels. And if this were not a myth, we could imagine him shrugging his shoulders to make his armor more comfortable before going out to battle.

And there are similar references to be found in other Sumerian tablets. These all unite to suggest that "thirty shekels worth" became an idiomatic expression implying that something (or someone) was either lightly esteemed or an object of contempt.

When this is applied to Judas, it explains why he was disinterested in the amount of money that was paid him by the chief priests. At heart, he had become so disgusted by Jesus' otherworldly views, that he now treated Him with contempt. The amount he asked the priests to give him revealed the depth of his disdain. The insignificance of the amount also made it easy for him to return the money to the priests (Matthew 27:3). It was so negligible that even his desire for riches was easily overcome by his feelings of remorse.

Archaeology makes an important contribution to our understanding of the Bible and human nature, and we want to make it easy for you to tap into the resources that are available. Not all "gems" lie on the surface waiting to be gathered. Some have to be quarried. What tools, therefore, will you need in order to be able to mine for these riches?

Among the books containing translations into English of ancient documents are: *Ancient Near Eastern Texts Relating to the Old Testament (ANET)*, edited by J. B. Pritchard (3d ed.; 1969/1992); *Ancient Records of Assyria and Babylonia (ARAB)*, edited by D. D. Luckenbill (2 vols.; 1926/1968), *Documents of Old Testament Times (DOTT)*, translated and edited by D. W. Thomas (1958), and *Near Eastern Religious Texts Relating to the Old Testament (NERT)*, translated by J. Bowden and edited by W. Beyerlin (1978).

But, with so much having been discovered, how can a person possibly keep at his or her fingertips the kind of data that will enhance his/her personal Bible study or add interest to the teaching of Scripture? To assist you in understanding what has been done, while also enabling you to keep pace with newer discoveries, reference can easily be made to *The Minister's Library*. In addition, two primary works will help you come to grips with information about the people and places of the ancient Near East. These are:

M. Avi-Yonah and E. Stein, eds., *Encyclopedia of Archaeological Excavations in the Holy Land* (now issued in a revised and enlarged edition under the title, *The New Encyclopedia of Archaeological Excavations in the Holy Land* with E. Stern and A. Lewinson-Gilboa serving as editors)

E. M. Blaiklock and R. K. Harrison , eds., *New International Dictionary of Biblical Archaeology*

The former is limited to Israel and its environs, while the treatment of the latter includes the lands of the "Fertile Crescent" as well as the countries surrounding the Mediterranean.

The *Encyclopedia of Archaeological Excavations in the Holy Land* (4 vols.; 1975-1978), and the *New Encyclopedia of Archaeological Excavations in the Holy Land* (4 vols.; 1993) were first published in Hebrew before they were translated into English. Both *EAEHL* and *NEAEHL* gather together information written by the world's foremost biblical archaeologists—much of which was previously dispersed in literally hundreds of books and journal articles. In discussing each site the contributors treat the history behind its identification as well as the history of its occupation through prehistoric, Bronze and Iron Ages, Persian and Hellenistic periods, and the era of the Crusades. Appropriate biblical references and supposed dates of occupancy are included in each article. Some questionable identifications (e.g., Ai, Debir) are not resolved.

Both *EAEHL* and *NEAEHL* are lavishly illustrated with color and black-and-white pictures of different artifacts, cross-sections of the excavations, and where appropriate, maps. The articles are signed, and brief bibliographies listing important books and/or essays are appended.

NEAEHL has now replaced *EAEHL* and it is indispensable to anyone interested in the history and geography, customs and culture of the peoples who have occupied the land of Israel. Its scope extends from the earliest human settlements to the Ottoman occupation, and covers investigations of sites on both sides of the Jordan River. Included is relevant data from Sinai to Elath in the south to the sources of the Jordan in the north. While coverage in *NEAEHL* includes all that appeared in EAEHL, other materials have been added to make *NEAEHL* as up-to-date as it is possible for a work to be. *NEAEHL* also contains information on monasteries, churches, and marine archaeology. There are also indexes of persons, places, and biblical references. *NEAEHL* will enrich the reading of the biblical narrative and add depth as well as interest to your research and knowledge of places you read about in the course of a careful perusal of the Scriptures. A list of contributors is to be found in volume 4.

The New International Dictionary of Biblical Archaeology, edited by E. M. Blaiklock and R. K. Harrison (1983), is a handy one-volume survey of the significant discoveries and their bearing on the study of Scripture. The articles are arranged alphabetically and each one is a masterpiece of condensed information. They cover topics ranging from "Aaron's Tomb" to "Ziusudra." Each site is identified, and where a location is difficult to pinpoint, alternate views are presented.

The treatment shows sensitivity to the progress of history and frequent reference is made to the writings of Josephus, Jerome, Eusebius, and others. Distances are given in both miles and kilometers. Each article is initialed and many of the articles contain important bibliographies. The *NIDBA* is a handy work and should occupy an important place among each Bible student's reference tools.

To date there are no online periodical indexes dedicated to Biblical archaeology. However, some Bible software packages allow key word searching of books on archaeology. For those who are interested in the Dead Sea Scrolls, however, there is the *Dead Sea Scrolls*, a multimedia, interactive CD-ROM (1994). The CD contains scroll photos with English translations, and covers the historical context and significance of the DSS through video clips, color photos, and interviews with scroll scholars.

Theological Reference Works

Theological reference works are numerous. They fall into two primary categories: *Biblical* and *Systematic*. Brief definitions of terms can be located in N. Turner's *Handbook for Biblical Studies* (1982), V. A. Harvey's *A Handbook of Theological Terms* (1976), and in T. L. Miethe's *Compact Dictionary of Doctrinal Words* (1988).

Biblical Theology

In general, biblical theology may be said to have a distinctive task. It builds upon the labors of the exegete who is, above all, a philologist and a historian. An exegete analyzes a word (e.g., "Covenant," "Grace") or a phrase (e.g., "Fear of the Lord," "Day of the Lord") to determine its usage in the cultural setting in which it was used. In this respect, a biblical theologian is like an architect. He or she takes the material supplied by the exegete/historian and strives to erect a harmonious structure in which each element of a word's usage and meaning is seen in its proper light and correct perspective.

Another aspect of biblical theology is to analyze the writings of a particular person (e.g., "Moses," "Paul," "Luke") and develop a "theology" that will explain each biblical writer's distinctive views in terms of a "Pentateuchal theology," or a "Pauline theology," or a "Lucan theology."

One of your initial preoccupations as a student of biblical theology will be with lexicons. You will need to combine exegesis with exposition so as to understand as accurately as possible the usage of words within a specific context. When the different nuances are understood in their varying time periods, and also in their relation to one another, you will be in a position to formulate these ideas into a presentation of the meaning of the word or phrase. Such an endeavor lays an essential foundation for the study of systematic theology.

The benefits of a sound biblical theology are many and include accuracy in handling the biblical text, a sense of authority in proclaiming it, and an inner quickening of your spirit as you begin, however falteringly, to realize how much God in Christ accomplished in our redemption. In addition, this approach to the actual words of Scripture helps expose non-biblical assumptions, recaptures the sense of unity of God's Word, and develops a norm or standard by which those who aspire to be biblical theologians are able to measure movements of the past as well as trends in the present.

Our aim in pursuing this line of investigation should be accuracy—accuracy in definition as well as accuracy in understanding the usage and meaning of a word or phrase, and the way in which this information contributes to our knowledge of doctrine. Such precision in interpretation should not lead to pride of heart but rather to humility as we all come to see and appreciate the matchless intricacy and marvelous consistency of God's progressive revelation. Specific resources may be traced through *The Minister's Library*.

In this section, we will discuss the following works. They are representative of the many volumes available on the subject.

A Vocabulary of the Bible, ed. J.-J. Von Allmen

Dictionary of Biblical Theology, ed. X. Leon-Dufour

Evangelical Dictionary of Biblical Theology, ed. W. Elwell

New International Dictionary of New Testament Theology, ed. C. Brown

Encyclopedia of Biblical Theology, ed. J. B. Bauer

Theological Dictionary of the New Testament, ed. G. Kittel and G. Friedrich

Theological Dictionary of the Old Testament, ed. G. J. Botterweck and H. Ringgren

New International Dictionary of Old Testament Theology and Exegesis, ed. W. A. VanGemeren

Theological Wordbook of the Old Testament, ed. R. L. Harris, G. L. Archer, Jr., and B. K. Waltke.

The *Vocabulary of the Bible*, edited by Jean-Jacques von Allmen (1958), was first translated into English in 1956 by P. J. Allcock et al., and was published under the title *Companion to the Bible*. It is the product of an evangelical Swiss Protestant theologian and a team of French and Swiss scholars. It was designed to serve the needs of students, ministers and laymen "seeking anew and rediscovering in the Holy Scriptures, the Word of the living God." In his Introduction to the English edition, H. H. Rowley remarked:

> In great periods of the history of the Church men knew what they believed, and a deeper theological interest today would lead to greater vitality in the Church. For theology is not something dull and remote, but something exciting and relevant. The Bible brings Good News to men, the stirring message of the wonder of God's love and the redemption whereby we can be lifted to share His life and power, and enter into His purpose for the world.[7]

Within the scope of this volume, therefore, we find alphabetically arranged articles from "Adoption" to "Worship." Each essay is signed, but bibliographies have been omitted from the English translation. In spite of their general brevity, insightful material is to be found in most of these studies. Especially significant is the treatment of "Covenant," "Cross," "Fear (including the 'fear of God')," "Image," "Law," "Man," "Marriage," et cetera. Surprisingly, articles on topics like atonement, propitiation, and theocracy are missing from this otherwise worthy compilation.

The Dictionary of Biblical Theology, edited by X. Leon-Dufour (4th ed., rev. and enlarged; 1995), was first published in French in 1962 under the title *Vocabulaire de theologie biblique* and has since attained a reputation in Roman Catholic as well as Protestant circles for its succinct scholarship.

A Jesuit priest by training, Leon-Dufour describes the purpose behind this present dictionary:

> Sacred Scripture is the Word of God to man; theology seeks to be the word of man about God. When theology limits its study to the immediate content of the inspired books, eager to listen to them in their own terms, to penetrate into their language--in brief, to become the precise echo of the Word of God--then theology is biblical in the strict sense of the term.[8]

While the editor speaks unashamedly of the divine inspiration of the Scriptures, many of the contributors are observed to hold to a variety of documentary theories. This is in spite of Leon-Dufour's having stated that the Bible possesses an amazing unity quite beyond the ability of man to develop. He also states that this "unity comes from the person who is its very center" (viz., Jesus Christ). Consequently, readers will find profound evangelical truths in these pages stated clearly and without ambiguity, and side by side other treatments of biblical truths that lamentably manifest a heavy reliance upon the tenets of theological "liberalism."

As far as the articles are concerned, each subject is well outlined and initialed. Many of them contain numerous cross-references, and each deals adequately with the broad parameters of the topic. The treatment of "Day of the Lord," "Faith," "Justification," "Mediator," "Pardon," "Redemption," "Truth," "Worship," and many more, is brief and helpful.

A table containing the abbreviations of books of the Bible (as found in the Douay Version) appears in the front of the dictionary with a list of the contributors. An "Analytical Table" of subjects dealt with is to be found at the end of the book together with a theological index.

The Evangelical Dictionary of Biblical Theology (1996), ed. W. A. Elwell is the product of evangelical Reformed theologians. It contains signed articles on over 500 different themes ranging from "Aaron" to "Zephaniah, Theology of." "See" references are used to good effect. Articles on "Hope," "Immorality, Sexual," and "Knowledge of God" are helpful. Some surprises are articles on "Education in Bible Times." "Law," and "Leadership." The articles on "Abortion" and "Homosexuality," however—two topics so crucial in today's milieu—stop short of being truly helpful.

All the articles are signed, and most of them contain bibliographies. The books cited in these bibliographies have, with few exceptions, been written from a theologically neo-orthodox or neo-liberal perspective. Inasmuch as the editor's preface stated that this work was for "most people" (and in particular those lacking knowledge in the original languages), the almost total absence of works written by conservative theologians is hard to understand. A very comprehensive Scripture index concludes this dictionary

The New International Dictionary of New Testament Theology, edited by C. Brown (3 vols. plus index; 1975-1978), is based upon the German *Theologisches Begriffslexikon zum Neuen Testament* by L. Coenen, E. Beyreuther and H. Bietenhard. This translation and revision brings within the grasp of the English reader a vast wealth of information pertaining to New Testament terminology and words of theological importance. The purpose behind the production of this work takes the form of an invitation to enter into the labors of others and delve into and begin to discover for oneself something of the limitless resources of God's inspired Word. The editor writes:

> A theological dictionary is not a collection of prepackaged sermons or an anthology of predigested devotion. It is more like an invitation to join in the collective enterprise of quarrying and building . . . (I Cor. 3:10ff.). It is as one quarries among the mass of data and tries to build something out of it that the data becomes alive. What was perhaps previously flat and feature-

less takes on new perspective and meaning. One can go even further. The great revivals of the Christian church have come about when some individual here and there has been grasped by something that his predecessors and contemporaries have taken for granted ....[9]

Arranged alphabetically according to the English word (e.g., "Baptism," "Child," "Disciple," "Exhort," "Grace") each article treats appropriate Greek words and their cognates. In ascertaining the meaning of the specific term under review, the contributor traces its usage through the classical period, probes its meaning in the Septuagint (LXX), and then deals with its occurrence in the New Testament. From this premise the reader is in a position to assess the theological significance of the word under consideration and relate the contribution of each biblical writer to the topic as a whole.

Each article is signed, and comprehensive bibliographies are to be found at the end of most articles. Separate subject indexes were provided for volumes 1 and 2, and a cumulated index of all articles appeared at the end of volume 3. These indexes have now been rendered obsolete with the issuing of a separate index volume. Each volume contains a "Table of Contents" listing the words treated. This is followed by a list of contributors citing the articles they wrote together with pertinent personal information. In addition, volume 1 contains a glossary of technical terms. For definitions of words that are frequently encountered in theological literature, this index is at once accurate and reliable. These volumes will provide indispensable insights to all who will take time to study them.

An Encyclopedia of Biblical Theology: The Complete Sacramentum Verbi, edited by J. B. Bauer (3 vols.; 1970/1981), originally appeared under the title *Sacramentum Verbi*. It was prepared with the Catholic lay person in mind and contains articles designed to cover topics associated with biblical theology from the perspective of the biblical writers. In doing so, it also makes available to readers a synthesis of the thinking of the leading theologians from the time of the apostles to the present.

The contributors realize that "dogmatic theology cannot be reduced to biblical theology," but rather must grow out of it. In each article, therefore, an attempt is made to allow the Scripture to speak for itself. It is interesting for Protestants to see to what extent the writers have been successful in their aim. In the article on the "Brethren of Jesus," for example, the contributor begins appropriately enough by listing those passages of Scripture where reference is made to Christ's "brethren." He then discusses the linguistics involved but concludes, in keeping with Catholic dogma, that these "brethren" must have been cousins of Jesus, not brothers and sisters.

While obviously slanted to the needs of Roman Catholics, this work should not be ignored by Protestants. The articles do manifest a theologically "liberal" stance, but this does not mean that topics like "Abraham," "Agape," "Authority," "Body," "Building up," "Conscience," "Conversion," "Day of Yahweh," "Death," et cetera, are devoid of value. Volume 1 contains the contents of all three volumes together with the author of each article.

G. Kittel and G. Friedrich edited the *Theological Dictionary of the New Testament*, translated and edited by G. W. Bromiley (9 vols. plus index; 18991903) Popularly referred to as either "Kittel" or *TDNT* (though cited as *TDNT* in the literature), this work is the product of outstanding German scholarship. The stance is decidedly "left of center," but the goal is "to elucidate every word of religious or theological significance in the New Testament." Included in the treatment are many proper names of people of importance (e.g., "Able," "Abraham," "Adam," etc.); a discussion of some prepositions of value in theological discussion; and a handling of words by their root forms together with cognate terms.

Each article appears with the Greek term(s) to be discussed clearly identified by being placed in a rectangular box. The word is then treated in keeping with its usage in classical times, the Old Testament (LXX), in Judaism, the New Testament, and finally the Apostolic and post-Apostolic periods. Handled in this way, the changes in meaning are clearly seen. Quotations from the Talmud, Midrash, Mishnah, or Greek writers of antiquity enhance the value of this work for research purposes.

All articles are signed, and a list of the contributors is to be found at the front of each volume. Extensive bibliographies conclude most essays. In spite of the lack of sympathy many of the contributors show toward evangelical approaches to the text, these studies are of inestimable value and should not be ignored.

Volume 10 contains indexes of English key words, Greek key words, and Aramaic and Hebrew words, and biblical references to both Testaments and the Apocrypha. It concludes with a list of the contributors and coworkers, giving, in addition to the date of birth and standing in the scholarly community, a list of their degrees and academic rank.

The *Theological Dictionary of the Old Testament*, edited by C. J. Botterweck and H. Ringgren, and translated by J. T. Willis (1974-in progress), is designed to be the companion of *TDNT*. Its discussion of key Old Testament words and concepts builds upon form-critical and traditio-historical methods of investigation. It also uses cognate languages (primarily Akkadian and Ugaritic) to bring to light the meaning of words found in the Old Testament whose etymology is often shrouded in antiquity.

Each article in *TDOT* treats the Hebrew terminology, surveys the occurrence of the word under consideration in Hebrew as well as in other Semitic languages, gives its equivalent in the Septuagint, and where applicable, its use in the Qumran (or Dead Sea) Scrolls, Pseudepigrapha, and Rabbinic literature. The result is a comprehensive discussion of the theological significance of each word, bringing before the researcher a wealth of material not otherwise easy to obtain.

The signed articles contain extensive footnotes. Hebrew words are transliterated in order to make the text more readable, and in many cases the meaning of foreign words is provided in the context. In those instances where the verses of the Masoretic Text differ from the verse divisions of the English Bible, the English verse is given in parenthesis. Scheduled for twelve volumes, this set has achieved "landmark" status.

The *New International Dictionary of Old Testament Theology and Exegesis*, ed. W. A. VanGemeren (5 vols.), has four main divisions: (1) The guide (1:1-218), contains specialized articles on such topics as hermeneutics, textual criticism, OT history, literary genre, narrative criticism, linguistics, principles of word study, OT theology, and more; (2) Lexical articles (1:219—4:343) consists of articles arranged according to Hebrew alphabet; (3) Topical dictionary (4:345-1322) including cross-references to the entries in the lexical section and discussing the names of people and places, words, concepts, and events; and (4) Indexes (5:1-834). Bibliographies for the longer articles direct users to other sources.

Of importance to *beginning* students is the *Theological Wordbook of the Old Testament*, edited by R. L. Harris, G. L. Archer and B. K. Waltke (2 vols.; 1981). *TWOT* follows a similar format to *TDOT*, and while it is less extensive and lacks an index (necessitating the use of James Strong's *Exhaustive Concordance of the Bible*), it is fairly complete and should be kept on one's reference shelf. It provides a concise handling of each Hebrew word and its cognates, and the synthesis given of all the relevant material makes the information easy to grasp. As a result, this should be one of the first works consulted by the busy pastor or the earnest Christian worker.

The explanation of the meaning of each word is related to the context in which it appears, and the explication of the theological concepts embodied in these words is unfolded in such a way as to enrich the user's understanding of God's self-disclosure of His will in the Old Testament. Each word, therefore, is treated in light of its etymology, cognate usage, and meaning in the *lingua franca* of the people. The result is an accurate, usable dictionary to the literature of the Old Testament. While some scholars will obviously differ with the contributors on minor matters, little divergence of opinion is likely to arise out of the definition assigned a given word.

Systematic Theology

Systematic theology is intimately intertwined with the history of ideas. Its roots are deeply embedded in the civilizations of the ancient world, antedating even the time of Abraham. In the progress of revelation, however, theology became identified with the revealed religions of Judaism and Christianity, and as the history of the church began to unfold it emerged as a distinct discipline. True theology, of necessity, should come from a study of the Bible itself. It should be grounded in exegesis and the exposition of the Scriptures, and then come to fruition as it interacts with other disciplines.

There has always been a danger that philosophy, dealing as it does with topics closely allied to theology, will unduly influence the "queen of the sciences" (instead of being influenced by it!). In recent years, and accompanying the erosion of the study in the original languages as a vital part of one's seminary studies, the basis of true systematics has been neglected. Today's theologians are seldom exegetes (as was B. B. Warfield), and often lack a sense of history. They are most often philosophers. This leads to the formulation of dogmas that are based on tradition and accepted uncritically. In time the beliefs of a group are seen to transcend even the teaching of Scripture (though adherents to a movement or denomination will often affirm that the Bible is the final authority in all matters of faith and practice).

As we evaluate reference tools in the broad area of theology we will need to do so in light of whether or not each article in a theological dictionary is based upon a demonstrated knowledge of the original languages and truly represents what the Bible has to say. In this connection we will consider together:

Evangelical Dictionary of Theology, ed. W. A. Elwell

Expository Dictionary of Bible Words, by L. O. Richards

Dictionary of Christian Theology, ed. A. Richardson

Sacramentum Mundi, ed. K. Rahner.

The *Evangelical Dictionary of Theology*, edited by Walter A. Elwell (1984) is, in reality, a revision and expansion of *Baker's Dictionary of Theology*, edited by E. F. Harrison et al (1960). Some of the articles of the earlier volume have been incorporated unchanged into the newer work, while other articles that are more germane to the study of the history of the church, have been added.

The *Evangelical Dictionary of Theology* is a companion volume to the *Evangelical Dictionary of Biblical Theology* (cited above). There is an overlap of some articles (e.g., "Names of God"), but the editor has wisely assigned these topics to different authors, thus allowing for interesting comparisons.

Informative treatments of different movements (e.g., "Albergenses," "Arians," "Montanists," "Nestorians," "Pelagians," etc.) make this book a handy resource. The overall emphasis, however, is slanted more toward Covenant/Reformed theology (as opposed to a theocratic[10] one), and so this imbalance predominates. The resultant tendency is to present conclusions without giving the reader an understanding of how these opinions were reached.

Valuable articles on "Adam, The Last," "Baptismal Regeneration," "Christology," "God," "Paul and Paulinism," and "Word" are worth consulting. Amillennial or post-millennial views appear to dominate most articles. The same criticisms made of Elwell's *Biblical Theology* apply here. A list of the contributors is to be found at the beginning of the work. The articles are signed, and most of the longer ones contain brief bibliographies. "See" and "See also" references are used judiciously.

The *Expository Dictionary of Bible Words*, by Lawrence O. Richards (1985) helps to make clear theological terms that may have begun to lose their meaning as a result of modern twentieth-century notions or concepts. Richards does a masterful piece of work in helping Bible students understand the original meaning of words like "Love," "Name," "Praise," "Ransom," the distinction between "Soul and Spirit," and much more. The result is the enrichment of one's study of the Scriptures as it comes to be understood in all the many facets of its meaning.

Users of this most helpful resource tool can expect to find a thorough coverage of both Old and New Testament terms; words common in the Authorized (King James) Version of the Bible clarified; and theological terms explained in light of their etymology—and all with a balance between an explanation of the practical truths of Scripture and the devotional life of the believer. Richards' work is complete with a Scripture index, subject index, and indexes to Hebrew and Greek words.

The *Dictionary of Christian Theology*, edited by Alan Richardson (1978), focuses the attention of the reader on contemporary theological issues. In its discussion of theological terms it leans heavily on the development of Christian ideas. First published in 1950, the early edition dealt mainly with words of doctrinal significance. Then, after nearly two decades, it was updated and expanded.

Arranged in alphabetical order, the topics treated cover just about everything from "*A Priori*" to "Zinzendorf" and "Abelard" to "Zwingli." Each article is signed, and helpful bibliographies conclude nearly all essays.

While no effort has been spared to secure the corroboration of some of the world's foremost scholars, few of them can be classified as either conservative or evangelical. Evidence of their scholarship, however, abounds, particularly in the succinct, descriptive statements about the meaning of Greek words, the biographical sketches of leaders in the church from the era of the Fathers to the present, and the evaluative critiques of sects and deviant religious movements. For the student seeking help in philosophy, there are also articles dealing with all the leading thinkers and their systems of thought.

It is as a work of theology that this dictionary, for all its merit, stands indicted. Biblical information supporting theological tenets is conspicuous by its absence. Having made this general observation, however, it still must be admitted that what is contained in these pages is of fine quality and evidences a high standard of scholarship.

Sacramentum Mundi: An Encyclopedia of Theology, edited by K. Rahner et al (6 vols.; 1968-1970), was designed for Roman Catholic laity, and was issued simultaneously in English, Dutch, French, German, Italian and Spanish. Its purpose was to articulate in modern-day terms the changes that have taken place within Catholicism since Vatican II. On examining the work we find that the contributors are all theologians of established repute; each article is signed; and bibliographies listing works in English, German, French, and occasionally Latin are appended to the longer essays. The topics treated run the gamut from "Absolute" to "Zionism." Most of them are well outlined.

The essay on "Temptation," however, is not as clear as some of the others, yet the progression of thought is well developed. Scripture references are numerous in part 2 of the writer's discussion, but philosophical considerations predominate in the introduction and conclusion. This article is illustrative of some of the weaknesses that are to be found in this work.

Important theologians (e.g., "Abelard," "K. Barth," "J. Calvin"); doctrines (e.g., "Empiricism," "Idealism," "Phenomenology"); topics (e.g. "Anointing of the Sick"), papal encyclicals; systems of ethics; pastoral ministry; and who are the "People of God," the "Roman Curia," and "Zen Buddhism," all find a place within these pages. Volume 6 contains a list of contributors and a general index.

LOOKING AHEAD

1. Trace as many articles as you can on the following topics: Decision-making, Leadership, Legitimacy/Illegitimacy, Maturity, Motivation, and the Puritans, in the following reference works:

Encyclopedia of Educational Research

International Encyclopedia of the Social Sciences.

How thorough is each treatment? What is the perspective of each writer (e.g., historical, philosophical, etc.)? Is the article well outlined? Signed? In comparing one article with another, apart from length, which do you prefer? Why?

2. Imagine that you are to research the lives and significant contribution(s) to education of each of the following: A. B. Bruce, J. B. Lightfoot, Mark Hopkins, and Roger Williams. A friend suggests that you consult the *Dictionary of American Biography* (*DAB*); and the *Dictionary of National Biography* (*DNB*).

   What report would you take back to your friend? How valuable were these works to you as you researched each person's life? Did you find any observable strengths and weaknesses in these reference tools? Be specific.

3. Consider the influence of Humanism, Idealism and Naturalism on education as found in the following reference works:

   Harper Dictionary of Religious Education

   Encyclopedia of Education.

   Who were the notable people involved in the spread of each viewpoint? What has been the contribution of each theory to education? How does each view differ from a distinctively Christian approach to education?

4. If you were to write a paper on the contribution of missions and missionaries to the education and sociology of a given race (i.e., one of your choice), what information could be derived from sources like . . .

   Concise Dictionary of the Christian World Mission

   Mission Handbook

5. How influential have Origen, Augustine, John Knox, William Penn, Thomas Arnold, and John Dewey been in shaping education trends (find out as much as you can from William Smith's *Dictionary of Christian Antiquities;* William Smith and Henry Wace's *Dictionary of Christian Biography, Literature, Sects and Doctrines;* as well as *DAC* and *DNB*).

4

General Reference Works
Part 3

RESOURCES TO ENRICH YOUR STUDY

Some years ago an advertisement appeared in several prominent business journals. In bold letters were the words: "SEND ME THE PERSON WHO READS." The ad went on to describe how an ill-informed person is a danger to himself and a menace to those who must rely upon him. This cord has been struck before. In the years before soap operas, sitcoms and sporting events brought into one's living room via television, John D. Snyder wrote *I Love Books* (1942). Toward the end of his work he penned the following words:

> The first step toward becoming an original thinker is to become familiar with the thoughts of others.... The man who never learns how to read will never become much of a thinker. When left alone, his mind is empty because he has not filled it with useful knowledge and can make no comparisons of ideas. When cast upon his own resources, he finds no reservoirs of thought within him to refresh his soul. Wide reading is the very foundation of ideas and constructive thinking, and the happiest person is one who thinks the most interesting thoughts.[11]

Since World War II there has come about an increasing emphasis on interdisciplinary studies. Old, "water-tight" compartments (e.g., law, medicine, philosophy, theology) have been compelled to interact with each other and integrate knowledge. This has sometimes resulted in the development of new disciplines like bioethics. Such integration of subject matter can either be resisted or welcomed. The fact remains that it is being done, and pioneers of the new discipline find the process to be rewarding and fulfilling. As a field of study grows information expands and changes. Our challenge is to learn how to access this information.

Theological research often takes us into fields of study that are based more on the truths found in the general revelation of God than special revelation. When this happens we should look for principles in God's Word that will keep us on track as we probe this new discipline. And sometimes we must rely on labels like "sacred' and "secular" when pursuing such knowledge, even though we may dislike this arbitrary dichotomy. In this chapter we will consider works that are primarily "secular" in nature. In our discussion we will treat a few areas as representative of the way in which you can engage in inter-disciplinary study. The subjects considered will be:

- Education
- History and Biography
- Missions
- Philosophy and Ethics
- Sociology and Psychology

Education

As you build upon the Scriptures to form a truly biblical approach to education, you may wish to broaden your reading by consulting some of the works listed in *The Minister's Library*. As you peruse the books recommended in *TML* you will be able to stand on the shoulders of those who have preceded you. Principles that "work" in secular areas, however, may not be biblical and you will need to exercise caution as you establish your own philosophy of education. To do this effectively, you will need to become cognizant of what the Bible teaches as well as be knowledgeable of modern theories of education. In this way you will be able to construct a Scriptural approach that will be relevant to the situation you face.

The first resource with which you will need to be familiar is *The Encyclopedia of Education*, edited by L. C. Deighton (9 vols. plus index; 1971). It comprises more than 1,000 scholarly, signed articles, and covers a variety of themes pertaining to institutions and people, processes and product, research and philosophy, history and theory, and the practices in vogue at different times in history.

Included in the *Encyclopedia of Education* is a discussion of public as well as private approaches to education, instruction techniques from preschool through graduate programs, and the nature and methods of learning. And for those who wish to become teachers, data is included on the role of governmental agencies, the value of special museums and libraries, and volunteer organizations.

Where appropriate, articles stress the *how to* of learning, as well as the *is* and the *ought*, and include the values to be acquired. No utopian models are suggested, but rather stress is placed upon the process of education that, ideally, should be lifelong.

While the history of some institutions is given, emphasis is laid upon educational systems within the United States. Issues of importance to academic institutions (e.g., accreditation, environment, library resources, etc.) are dealt with clearly and concisely. Matters of importance to those who teach within these institutions (e.g., academic freedom, tenure) are also discussed.

Of general interest to those earning degrees are articles like "Academic Regalia," "Accrediting Agencies," "Adult Education," "Role of the Library," "Degrees, Academic," and much more. Other significant articles deal with the place of the emotions in education, ethics, the goals of education, studies in human potential, the classification of knowledge, and a multitude of other topics. Readers will find that each article has been well outlined and bibliographies have been appended to most entries. Valuable treatments of "Libraries, Academic" and special resources (e.g., *ERIC—Educational Resources Information Center*) together with critiques of journals and biographical sketches of leading educators, make this a volume worthy of continuous consultation. The time spent browsing through the index volume will readily alert you the wealth of important material available.

On a broader scale is the *International Encyclopedia of Higher Education*, edited by A. S. Knowles (10 vols.; 1977). Volume 1 is devoted to a detailed, alphabetically arranged table of contents, together with a list of contributors and the institutions they serve. This is followed by a section on "Acronyms" and a glossary. Prominent within these pages is the access of minorities to higher education, the international admissions process, continuing adult education (with patterns of organization and collaboration), the special demands of different disciplines (e.g., agriculture, engineering), the scope of education in countries outside the U.S.A. (e.g., the Arab world, Argentina, etc.), and Christian schools and colleges in different areas.

The articles are signed and conclude with comprehensive bibliographies. Volume 10 contains name and subject indexes. The latter warrants perusal and may be suggestive of topics to be fleshed out in papers, theses, or dissertations.

Not to be overlooked is the *Encyclopedia of Educational Research*, edited by M. C. Alkin (6th ed.; 4 vols., 1992). Now updated from the 5th (1982) edition, these volumes provide researchers with a synthesis of research. They contain 257 comprehensive alphabetically arranged, signed articles by 325 contributors. The articles vary in length and include new topics like teen mothers, and AIDS education. Cross-references abound. Included are informative tables and excellent bibliographies. Well-indexed.

In religious education, and replacing the *Encyclopedia of Sunday Schools and Religious Education* (1915) and the *Westminster Dictionary of Christian Education* (1963), is *Harper's Encyclopedia of Religious Education* (1990), edited by I. V. Cully and K. B. Cully, and E. L. Towns' *Towns' Sunday School Encyclopedia* (1992).

The work by Cully and Cully is an interfaith encyclopedia that contains articles written by men and women of all denominations, including some of Jewish and Moslem persuasions. What is presented here, though liberal in its orientation, may nevertheless be consulted with profit by those engaged in undergraduate as well as some graduate programs.

Towns' Sunday School Encyclopedia is entirely different from those just mentioned. Its 639 pages contain what the publishers claim is "all you need to know about the Sunday school." Topics are treated alphabetically; job descriptions are provided; recent trends are discussed; effective teaching methods are explained; policy statements relating to difficult cases are mentioned; and effective new methods and strategies (for age groups such as "baby boomers" and "yuppies") are included. All things considered, this is a valuable resource.

History and Biography

A knowledge of who did what and when and where will go a long way toward filling in the gaps in one's thinking and infusing new vitality into one's research for traditional courses. This is particularly true when it comes to the progress of Christianity through the centuries. Such study has often been found to rejuvenate courses like the "History of Christian Thought."

We will begin our review of available resources with *A Dictionary of Christian Biography, Literature, Sects and Doctrines*, edited by William Smith and Henry Wace (4 vols.; 1877). It continues Smith's famous *Dictionary of the Bible* (4 vols.; 1865, that was revised and ed. by H. B. Hackett in 1896 and reprinted in 1981), and contains "in the form of a biographical dictionary a complete collection of materials for the history of the Christian church from the time of the Apostles to the age of Charlemagne."

Many of the articles are long. They are all initialed, and brief bibliographies conclude some of the more important ones. Other references and quotations are frequently found in the body of an article. The contributors are all 19th-century theologians and historians, and include in their number individuals such as C. J. Ellicott, E. Hatch, F. J. A. Hort, J. B. Lightfoot, W. Milligan, H. C. G. Moule, G. Salmon, A. P. Stanley, H. B. Swete, B. F. Westcott, and C. Wordsworth, together with host of other lesser-known luminaries.

Important discussions of great leaders of antiquity include lengthy articles on "Athanasius," "Augustine," "Bar-Cochba," "Beda (Bede)," "Carpus," "Celsus," "Cerinthus," and of course, "Charlemagne." Doctrinal essays include the "Antichrist," "Arianism," "Baptism," "Christology," "Church," "Confession," "Death and the Dead," "Demonology" and "Docetism." Historical discussions begin with the "Apologists," "Apostolic Fathers," "Balaamites," "Cabbalah," "Conscience," "Coptic Church and church creeds," et cetera, and continue through the first nine centuries A.D. Their fullness of detail will astound the reader. All of this makes the *Dictionary of Christian Biography* a valuable resource. In point of fact, these four volumes comprise a work of such massive scholarship that those who neglect them do so to their detriment.

An abridged one volume edition with the title *A Dictionary of Christian Biography and Literature to the End of the Sixth Century* by H. Wace and W. C. Piercy, was published in 1911 and reprinted in 1994. It contains only the most important biographies found in the larger, four volume edition.

The *Dictionary of Christian Antiquities*, edited by William Smith and Samuel Cheetham (2 vols.; 1876), is fully in keeping with the high standard of scholarship attained by this Oxford scholar and his colleagues as reflected in the works just mentioned. And it gives evidence of the same painstaking care that made his other publications famous. Sir William intended it to supplement the *Dictionary of Christian Biography, Literature, Sects, and Doctrines* and the *Dictionary of Christian Antiquities*, and in the present volumes treat "the organization of the Church, its officers, legislation, discipline, and revenues; the social life of Christians; the worship of the early church, its ceremonies, music, vestments, instruments and insignia; sacred places; architecture and other forms of art; symbolism; sacred days and seasons, and the graves or Catacombs in which some believers were laid to rest."

While also covering the period from the death of the Apostles to the time of Charlemagne, these volumes contain informative insights into the social life of people living during these centuries (as seen in articles on "Actors and Actresses," "Books, Censure of," "Catacombs," "Contract of Marriage," "Dancing," "Divination," "Fasting," etc.); church rites and practices ("Baptism," "Confession," the rise of the office of "Bishop," "Celibacy," "Council,"); social attitudes and customs (e.g., "Adultery," "Betrothal," "Burial of the Dead," "Family," "Marriage"); events in the Christian year (e.g., "Advent," "Ascension Day," "Calendar," "Easter," "Holy Week," etc.); notable councils of the church (at Alexandria, Antioch, Chalcedon, Constantinople, Nicea); and much, much more.

The wealth and variety of information to be found in these volumes, together with their fullness and accuracy, places the researcher forever in the debt of those whose assiduous studies and arduous labor made this work possible. Whether investigating the development of church government or the origins of ritual, the practice of cultic groups or the fate of martyrs, or studying marriage and the family or the relationship of parents to children, all is recorded here with a completeness and precision that is without equal today.

Extensively documented; each article is also initialed. A list of the contributors is to be found in volume 1.

The following encyclopedic works will also reward your research while at the same time adding depth to your knowledge of the great men and women who have preceded you. The first is the *Dictionary of National Biography*, edited by Leslie Stephen and Sidney Lee (21 vols., 1938- , plus supplements). It is a work of such scholarship that it set the standard for dictionaries of this kind throughout the world. While excluding living persons, it included notable English men and women both in the United Kingdom and throughout the British Empire (including Americans of the Colonial Period). Supplements issued from 1912 to the present have kept *DNB* up to date. While not all articles are of equal value, in many instances this is the only resource available when seeking for reliable information about notable people. And where Christianity is concerned, *DNB* is inclined to be more objective than its American counterpart.

DNB's coverage includes the life and contribution of an educator of the caliber of Thomas Arnold; distinguishes between clergymen who bear the same name (e.g., John Brown of Haddington, John Brown of Whitburn, and John Brown of Edinburgh); includes Catholics as well as Protestants (e.g., Frederick William Faber, and F. W. Farrar); high churchmen such as J. B. Lightfoot and B. F. Westcott as well as independents like Robert Haldane and William Kelly.

A reprint with revisions to 1950 is entitled *Dictionary of National Biography: The Concise Dictionary* (2 vols.; 1953-1961). This *Concise Dictionary* also contains an index to the larger work. Other supplements have also been issued, keeping this unique resource up-to-date. (A word of caution: the print is very small. You'll need a magnifying glass to read it.)

The *Dictionary of American Biography*, edited by Allan Johnson (20 vols., 1928-37; plus supplements in 8 volumes, issued in 1944-88, and a comprehensive index in 1990), is designed to supply in the United States the counterpart of the *Dictionary of National Biography* in the United Kingdom. It contains approximately 14,000 articles of noteworthy, though deceased, American men and women, and serves as a valuable resource tool for all who are studying the impact of individuals on social life and culture. Prominent people from all walks of life and all religious and non-religious backgrounds have been included (e.g., William Jennings Bryan, Robert Ingersoll, James Russell Lowell, Ira D. Sankey, George Washington Carver, and many more).

Some of the articles are of considerable length. They have all been contributed by noted scholars, are signed, and contain bibliographies.

DAB is ideally suited to your needs should you wish to read up on a leader about whom separate biographies may not be readily available. One word of caution: In a few instances the biographer appears to lack empathy with his or her subject.

The more comprehensive *National Cyclopedia of American Biography* (63 vols.; 1892/1977) has as its stated purpose the creation of a biographical record of men and women within the United States who are deemed worthy of rank with the great leaders of Europe. Included are photographic reproductions or sketches of these individuals—statesmen, soldiers, clergymen, lawyers, writers, artists, scientists, et cetera. These people contributed in the broadest sense to the heritage and culture that we now enjoy. *NCAB* ceased publication in 1984.

As we take a closer look at *NCAB* we find that volume 1 provides a list of the contributors together with their credentials. Then, beginning with George Washington biographies of other notable men and women are given a place in this unique record. A strict chronological sequence is followed, and this makes the use of the comprehensive alphabetic index to volumes 1—62 and the Current Series (which updates the work, *viz.*, Vols. A—M and N—63) a necessity. This index volume was issued in 1984. *NCAB* may well be regarded as an indispensable resource!

The New International Dictionary of the Christian Church, edited by J. D. Douglas (1974; revised ed., 1978), is designed to give readers "a renewed sense of history; an identification and feeling of fellowship with those who have carried the torch before them; ... and most of all an appreciation of the priceless heritage which is ours in Christ." Limited to one volume, *NIDCC* is the product of a team of international scholars. You will find in these signed articles a treatment of subjects both old and new. In some instances, articles on historical movements well known in the annals of Christendom have been treated concisely and fairly (e.g., the "Clapham Sect," the Ecumenical Movement, etc.). At other times, however, subjects have been discussed all too briefly, and this does little to dispel the mists of obscurity that have enshrouded them (e.g., the "Five Mile Act," etc.).

The biographical sketches treat the better known leaders of Christendom (e.g., "Jonathan Edwards," "Charles Hodge," "C. T. Studd"), as well as a few of the lesser known individuals whose lives have made an impact for good or ill on the Christian church (e.g., "Pope Joan," "J. Kitto," "R. Lull," "E. B. Pusey"). In some instances these sketches have been accompanied by an evaluative critique of their theology (as, for example, in the case of "J. W. Colenso," "W. R. Inge," "R. Kittel," "C. Spalatin"). But certain lamentable omissions are evident. No mention is made of Charles C. Gordon, the famous British general who did so much to provide a foothold for the spread of the Gospel in the lands in which he served; or of Karl H. Graf who, with Julius Wellhausen, gave impetus to negative biblical criticism through the popularization of the "Documentary Hypothesis" of the Pentateuch; or of John M. Gregory, one-time president of the University of Illinois and a Christian educator *par excellence*; or of Granville Sharp whose indefatigable labors ultimately brought to an end the slave trade.

While each essay is short, brief bibliographies have been appended to some of them. Lamentably, these bibliographies do not always cite the best works!

Among the other works that J. D. Douglas has edited, are *Who's Who in Christian History* (1992) and the *Twentieth Century Dictionary of Christian Biography* (1995). The former provides brief biographies of more than 1,500 men and women whose lives made a lasting impact on Christianity. The latter, though a valiant effort, is disappointing. Among its glaring omissions are C. L. Feinberg, Roberta Hestenes, Josh McDowell and Warren W. Wiersbe. John Wimber is mentioned, but not Chuck Smith.

Other works of a similar genre include *The Oxford Dictionary of the Christian Church*, edited by F. L. Cross and E. A. Livingstone (1977); *The Westminster Dictionary of Church History*, edited by J. C. Bauer (1971); and Elgin S. Moyer's *Wycliffe Biographical Dictionary of the Church*, edited by E. E. Cairns.

The *Oxford Dictionary of the Christian Church* is slanted more toward the history of the Anglican (Episcopal) Church in England. The articles are brief but factual, though undeniably leaning toward Anglo-

Catholicism and theological liberalism. Prominence is given those issues related to the observance of days and rituals. The bibliographies are brief and list the most scholarly works.

Bauer's *Westminster Dictionary of Church History* pays more attention to churches and church organizations in the United States. Only the most prominent of evangelicals receive mention (e.g., "Jonathan Edwards," "D. L. Moody"). The emphasis is on externals (rites, ceremonies). The bibliographies are brief.

Of greater help is E. S. Moyer's *Who Was Who in Church History* (1968). It has now been revised and edited by E. E. Cairns and issued under the title *Wycliffe Biographical Dictionary of the Church* (1982). It covers the whole of church history, is interdenominational in scope, and introduces readers to over 2,000 men and women—famous and infamous—from all over the world. A few lamentable omissions occur, for example, there is no mention of Thomas J. Jackson or of Brendan the Navigator.

Of a slightly different sort is J. Gordon Melton's valuable *Biographical Dictionary of American Cult and Sect Leaders* (1986). Being able to identify cult and sect leaders is most advantageous, particularly in the age of pluralism in which we live. Melton's work, therefore, is a major contribution to understanding the leaders themselves as well as the groups they founded or led. Included are representatives from Baha'i, Buddhist, Hindu, Islamic, Rosicrucian, and Shintoist faiths. A few of the surprises include Menno Simons and J. N. Darby, J. Frank Norris and J. Gresham Machen.

Appendixes contain lists of leaders by sect, birthplace, and belief. All things considered, this is an important reference work.

Missions

The carrying out of the "Great Commission" is the mission of the church. What has been done, as well as what remains to be done, may be gleaned from *A Concise Dictionary of the Christian World Mission*, edited by S. Neill, G. H. Anderson and J. Goodwin (1971). The editors called upon a group of well-trained missiologists to treat the rise and progress of missions from 1492 to the present. Focusing upon all the countries of the world, they provided biographies of notable leaders, and dealt with topics ranging from "Acculturation" to "Witchcraft." Though now dated, the contributors succeeded in placing before the reader a fine digest of missionary work and practice

More than 200 men and women contributed articles to this dictionary. Inasmuch as they came from all the countries of the world, this work may be said to be truly international. Because all denominations are represented, the end product may also be classified as truly ecumenical. Their articles vary in length. All are signed. The longer ones contain bibliographies. "See" references are to be found in the body of an article, not at the end.

More up-to-date, and serving as a worthy supplement, is the work edited by G. H. Anderson entitled *Biographical Dictionary of Christian Missions* (1998).

Up to date statistical and cultural information may be obtained from MARC's *Mission Handbook* (15th ed.; 1993-1995), supplemented by the 16th ed. (1996) and now, in the 17th edition (1998) brought up to date in *Mission Handbook 1998-2000*, edited by J. A. Siewert and E. G. Valdez. It serves as a directory of missionary organizations, et cetera. Initiated by the Missions Advanced Research and Communication Center, this book has become one of the leading resources of data for Protestant missionaries. Also worthy of consultation is MARC's earlier *Mission Handbook: North American Protestant Ministries Overseas* (4 vols.; 1973-1981), and the *Mission Handbook: USA/Canada Protestant Ministries Overseas,* edited by W. D. Roberts and J. A. Siewert (in process; 1989-) which continues the *North America Protestant Ministries Overseas* series.

Less up to date is the *World Christian Handbook* (1949) by H. W. Casual and K. Grubb. However, annuals published by Europa (e.g., on *Africa South of the Sahara, The Far East and Australasia, The Middle East and North Africa,* etc.), provide aspiring missiologists with a wealth of pertinent information.

Also of help to the researcher are the *area handbooks* issued by the Superintendent of Documents, U. S. Government Printing Office. They give easy access to essential information about the countries of the world (e.g., "Costa Rica," "Ecuador," "Egypt," "Korea," "Pakistan," "Somalia") with information that is of great importance to aspiring missiologists. They are revised and updated at intervals.

Several Internet sites are excellent sources for current statistical and cultural information about countries. The Library of Congress, in conjunction with its Country Studies/Area Handbook Series [1cweb2.loc.gov/frd/cs/cshome.html], provides extensive country profiles that are searchable by keyword. Two other federal government sites that provide less extensive information are the U. S. Department of State Country Background Notes [www.state.gov/www/background_notes/index.html] and The World Factbook [www.odci.gov/cia/publications/factbook/index.html] published annually by the Central Intelligence Agency. One of the most helpful is the Infonation [www.un.org/Pubs/CyberSchoolBus/

infonation/e_infonation] web site. It provides statistical data on United Nations member countries. Internet subject directories such as Yahoo [www.yahoo.com] and Britannica Internet Guide [www.britannica.com] give current country information that can be found under the subject headings "Countries" or "World Geography and Culture" or by keyword searching.

Though now showing signs of its advanced age, *The Encyclopedia of Modern Christian Missions: The Agencies*, edited by B. L. Goddard et al (1967), sets a pattern for other works to follow. It was produced by the faculty of the Gordon Divinity School, Massachusetts, and made available essential information (e.g., address, income, history, number of workers, nature of missionary enterprise, projects and literature describing the work) to 1,437 primarily Protestant agencies carrying on missionary work in all parts of the world. As such, it dealt with "missions" in its widest sense.

Articles were all numbered and signed, and ranged form "Aoh Church of God" to the "Zurich Mission Fur Sud--Und Osteuropa." Indexes providing "Letter Designation of Agencies" (e.g., Place, *Japan*; Type, *Literature and Bible Distribution*) make this an ideal resource tool for students engaged in researching different kinds of missionary enterprise in different parts of the world.

For additional information see *The World Directory of Mission Related Educational Institutions*, compiled by R. B. Baker, Sr., and T. Ward (1972), and the *World Directory of Missionary Training Programmes: A Catalog of Over 500 Missionary Training Programmes from Around the World*, edited by R. V. J. Windsor (1995).

Philosophy and Ethics

Integration is incomplete without the application of truth to life. Philosophy contains the attempts of different people to uncover truth, and ethics reflects the attempts of the same or different people to provide a rational basis for conduct. Both of these disciplines are intimately related to theology, so much so that many contemporary exponents of morality are often both philosophers and theologians. (We should always bear in mind, however, that a true theologian is first and foremost an exegete. He or she should build a system of knowledge upon the Word of God. Only then may information from other disciplines be compared with the teaching of Scripture.)

The Encyclopedia of Philosophy, edited by Paul Edwards (8 vols.; 1967/1996), is a work that deals extensively with Eastern and Western philosophy; ancient, medieval and modern writers; and the theories of mathematicians, physicists, biologists, sociologists, moral reformers and religious thinkers. The 1,500 signed articles are all well outlined and contain extensive bibliographies. Researchers will also find that this work abounds with information about philosophers (e.g., Barth, Nietzsche, Tillich); philosophies (historical, metaphysical, pragmatic, religious); philosophical movements (Communism, Hegelianism, Pragmatism); and religious ideologies and ideas (Gnosticism, Pietism).

The zealous inquirer will also find within these pages a plethora of data to filter through his or her thought processes--data, for example, on "Agnosticism," "Aquinas," "Atheism," "Augustinianism," ""Bernard of Clairvaux," "Causation," "Conscience," "Determinism," "Doubt," "Epicureanism," ethical theories, "Evil," and, of course, the list could go on and on.

Of significance is the fact that the articles include biographies as well as descriptions of different movements. The writings of the leading men and women discussed receive close, objective scrutiny; evaluative comments are included, and stimulus is provided for further research.

An article on "Philosophical Dictionaries and Encyclopedias" (VI:170-199) alerts users to other source materials. A supplement was released in 1996.

Worthy of consultation is the work edited by L. C. Becker and C. B. Becker entitled an *Encyclopedia of Ethics* (2 vols.; 1992). It is essentially a philosophical reference work containing 435 signed articles contributed by 260 scholars. The length of the articles varies from 500 to 9,000 words (with seventy per cent being between 1,000 and 5,000 words). Bibliographies conclude each article, and cross-references and "see also" references supplement the subject and author indexes. Of special interest are the perceptive essays treating topics like "Civil Rights and Civil Duties" and "Common Good," "Pride," and "Suicide." Also worth of consultation are the biographical sketches discussing "Bertrand Russell," "Rene Descartes," "John Dewey," and "Ludwig Wittgenstein."

Some of the articles overlap into the area of psychology (e.g., "Self-deception." and "Self-respect," "Guilt and Shame"), and it is natural to expect biographical treatments of men and women like "William James," "Karen Horney," and "Soren Kierkegaard" in this work.

Extensive articles of significance to missiologists and students of comparative religions include the ethical systems of different countries (e.g., Japan) and non-Christian religions (e.g., Islam).

There is a lot to be gained from these volumes, even though the perspective is entirely secular.

A notable addition to this subject is the *Blackwell Encyclopedia of Modern Christian Thought*, edited by A. E. McGrath (1993). It is the product of 93 contributors with only 12 being from countries other than the U.K. and U.S.A. The result is a one-volume work that focuses primarily on the Occidental world, even though articles on "Black Theology' and "Indian Christian Thought" do attempt to give balance to it as an encyclopedia.

The bulk of *Blackwell's Encyclopedia* is made up of long, thematic articles, supplemented by shorter ones that focus on people of ancient and modern times. Lacking is information about the devil, heaven, or hell. (Perhaps modern philosophers have found these to be an unnecessary part of the belief structure of modern people.) Illustrations of the kind of treatments given philosophers in this encyclopedia are the articles on John Hick and Francis Schaeffer. At opposite ends of the theological spectrum, Hick is dealt with in a powerful polemic that refutes the basis of his views, while Schaeffer is treated more kindly.

As in all works of this nature, there are some surprises. The article on "The Problem of Evil" shares a heading on the same page as "Evangelism." The volume concludes with a helpful index.

Other works of varying merit include Simon Blackburn's *Oxford Dictionary of Philosophy* (1996); the *Cambridge Dictionary of Philosophy* (1995); Thomas Mautner's *A Dictionary of Philosophy* (1996); and William L. Reese's *Dictionary of Philosophy and Religion: Eastern and Western Thought* (1996).

Of interest to you in the whole process of integration will be the *Encyclopedia of Biblical and Christian Ethics*, edited by R. K. Harrison (1987). Notable articles deal with "Choice," "Freewill" and "Determinism." In addition, a lengthy treatment entitled "Christian Ethics, History" ably introduces readers to the variety of beliefs held by different individuals during the past two millennia. While some of the articles are disappointing (e.g., "Fear" which omits the "fear of the Lord" motif that is so prominent in the ethics of both Old and New Testaments), others are too brief to be of lasting significance (e.g., "Envy," "Eros," "Greed"). Certain others, however, are most helpful (e.g., "Ecology," ""Education and Morality," ""False Witness," etc.).

If it is borne in mind that this work was produced in an era of moral ambivalence and confusion over values, then perhaps aspiring ethicists can build upon the foundation laid in the contributors and, through their own efforts, refine our understanding of ethical distinctions.

The contributors are mentioned at the beginning of this work and they are cited by their initials at the bottom of the articles they wrote. Those entries not bearing the initials of a contributor are presumed to be the editor's. Helpful bibliographies conclude some of the longer articles. These are not necessarily representative of the different viewpoints, and so users of this work will need to augment their research with a wider variety of resources.

The Dictionary of Christian Ethics, edited by J. Macquarrie (1967), differs dramatically from the work edited by R. K. Harrison. It manifests concern over the evident lack of a realization of any moral obligation or consciousness of "sin." To meet a felt need, therefore, the editor solicited articles from leading Reformed scholars (mainly Episcopalians and Presbyterians) in the U.S.A. and U.K. Each contributor was required to deal realistically with the complexities of the subject assigned to him or her. The result is a "guide to Christian ethics, not in the sense of laying down rigid norms, but in the sense of letting the reader see what the problems are, letting him know what the leading Christian moralists are thinking about the problems, and so [hopefully] enable him to come to his own intelligent and responsible decisions."

Each article is signed, and the major ones contain bibliographies.

In evaluating the strengths and weaknesses of this dictionary, let it first be admitted that, in treating this contribution objectively, the writers have drawn fine philosophical distinctions between beliefs and values, duty and desire, experience and practice, et cetera. In addition, excellent discussions of the leading philosophers and their systems of thought are to be found within these pages. Furthermore, Jewish, Buddhist, non-Christian sects, and even Communistic ethics have been treated with scholarly acumen.

In the final analysis, however, little use has been made of the Scriptures as the revelation of the will of God to man. At best, therefore, what is to be found within these pages is an appeal to external norms as opposed to an internal dynamic that can bring an individual's life into conformity with the truth of the Word of God.

In further developing your integrative ideas you may wish to consult: *Dictionary of Ethics, Theology and Society*, edited by P. A. B. Clarke and A. Linzey (1996); the *Encyclopedia of Bioethics*, edited by W. T. Reich (rev. ed.; 1995); and the *Encyclopedia of Ethics*, edited by L. C. Becker and C. B. Becker (2 vols.; 1992).

Sociology and Psychology

Accompanying the "relational revolution" there is now an emphasis on ministering to the whole person. Such an approach is biblical. The "relational revolution," however, minimized the need for biblical distinctions and emphasized instead mankind's existential needs. In the process, however, this approach has sown the seeds of its own demise and in time will reap the results of its lack of biblical orthodoxy.

In assessing the literature on these related subjects you would be negligent if you failed to capitalize on the strengths of others and did not expand your ministry to apply the "whole council of God" (Acts 20:27) to the moral and spiritual, social and ethical needs of those to whom you minister. Lamentably, this is where many evangelicals fall short.

The following general reference works are representative of the many scholarly books available at the present time.

The *International Encyclopedia of Psychiatry, Psychology, Psycho-Analysis, and Neurology*, edited by B. B. Wolman (12 vols.; 1977. Progress vols. 1983-), contains much that pastors engaged in an extensive counseling ministry (or students pursuing the study of human nature) will find valuable. Over 1,500 authors contributed articles to this encyclopedia. Coverage includes an objective description of the status of research followed by a discussion of the different methods of counseling. Frequent cross-references are found, and most articles contain bibliographies.

Obviously, you will not be expected to agree with all of the ideas or opinions expressed by those whose articles you may consult. In this encyclopedia, however, there is such an abundance of information (covering topics like "Adolescence," "Aged," "Cognition," "Communication." "Death," "Depression," "Emotions," "Family," "Father," "Group Dynamics," "Leadership," "Mass Media," etc.) that you will find your mental processes stimulated whether you agree with the viewpoint of the writer or not.

Of significance is the extensive discussion of "Marriage." In addition to describing current social mores, there is also a discussion of the origins and development of marital conflict. Then the various theories of conflict resolution are outlined together with an analysis of changing family roles. Helpful evaluations of each theory and method of counseling conclude each section.

Biographical sketches of deceased psychologists or psychiatrists enhance the overall usefulness of this work. Volume 12 contains the indexes that include an alphabetic listing of the contents of volumes 1--12; a name index citing where a significant person's work is mentioned; and a helpful subject index leading the earnest inquirer to all the places where his or her topic is treated.

The *International Encyclopedia of the Social Sciences*, edited by David L. Sills and Robert K. Merton (19 vols.; 1991)—while similar in scope to the *Encyclopedia of the Social Sciences* (15 vols.; 1930-1935)—is designed to complement rather than supplement its predecessor. Articles cover all aspects of sociology including anthropology, economics, geography, history, law, political science, psychiatry, psychology and statistics.

With articles arranged alphabetically by topic (as opposed to being arranged under each of the above mentioned disciplines) and with specific articles sharing the same general subject matter being grouped together, the use of the index (vol. 19) is essential.

Biographical articles of approximately 600 scholars (including "John Calvin," "Martin Luther") have been included, together with sociological articles on all the major religions (e.g., "Islam," "Judaism"), the role of Monasticism, and the relationship of Negativism to Revivalism. Other excellent articles cover "Aging," "Leadership" (including its psychological, sociological and political aspects), "Loyalty," "Marriage," "Near Eastern Society," and much more.

A list of the contributors together with an alphabetic listing of articles, a classification of each article under broad headings, and a general index are to be found in volume 19.

This is an indispensable work, and a few minutes spent perusing the index will be sufficient to spark the imagination of the alert reader to a variety of topics where secular research can be compared to biblical teaching.

Sociology of People in Bible Lands

Two of the most popular works for Bible students are Roland deVaux's *Ancient Israel: Its Life and Institutions*, translated by J. McHugh (1961), that was subsequently divided into two sections and published in two volumes, and Johannes Pedersen's *Israel: Its Life and Culture* (4 vols. in 2; 1959). Both books contain a "goldmine" of valuable information.

The Harper Encyclopedia of Bible Life, by Madeline S. Miller and J. Lane Miller (3d ed., revised by B. M. Bennett, Jr., and D. H. Scott; 1982), is arranged topically under three major headings: "The World of the Bible," "How the People of the Bible Lived," and "How the People of the Bible Worked." It has received the praise of scholars of all persuasions, but manifests a decidedly liberal bias, which mitigates against its overall reliability.

The third edition differs from previous editions, which consisted of sections arranged alphabetically by topic. Now the arrangement makes the work less easy to use. It does have the advantage, however, of being more up to date. It is not encyclopedic (as the title would tend to indicate), and the lengthy essays bear more of a relationship to Roland de Vaux's *Ancient Israel* than to an "encyclopedia" of Bible life.

As with the previous editions, this work is beautifully illustrated. In spite of these weaknesses this reference volume is of value if used with discernment.

A related resource is by W. Corswant and bears the title, *A Dictionary of Life in Bible Times* (translated by A. Heathcote; 1960). It, too, may also be consulted with profit.

LOOKING AHEAD

In preparation for the more specialized reference works to be covered in the next chapter--works dealing with: (1) places mentioned in the Bible; (2) commentaries expounding the Bible; and (3) concordances to the Bible; consider the following portions of Scripture, focus your investigation on:

- David being forced to flee for his life from the presence of King Saul (1 Samuel 20--27)
- The statement of the Lord Jesus in Luke 4:18-19; and the Apostle Paul's usage of the word "law."

1. By consulting the Bible atlases mentioned in an earlier chapter, trace (a) David's journeys from Gibeah to Ramah, and eventually to Gath and Ziklag; and (b) the footsteps of the Lord Jesus back to Nazareth following His baptism by John. Where is the traditional site of His temptation?

   Which of these atlases did you find most helpful? When would you use it? What are the strengths and weaknesses of these works?

2. By consulting "law" in Strong's *Exhaustive Concordance of the Bible* and the *New American Standard Exhaustive Concordance of the Bible*, determine how frequently the Apostle Paul used the word in each of his epistles? Where is its usage most common? Is its meaning always the same? How would you distinguish between references to (a) the moral law, (b) the Law of Moses, and (c) the Books of the Law? As you compare these concordances, which do you prefer? Why?

3. The quotation from Isaiah appearing in the context of Luke 4:14-21 can validly by researched in both Testaments. What did Christ omit when He quoted the passage from Isaiah? By using commentaries of your choice, summarize the reasons for the omission (as given by the respective commentators). Why do *you* believe the omission to be significant? What are your reasons?

5

Important Resources for Bible Study

In his introduction to the *Ryrie Study Bible*, Dr. Charles C. Ryrie commented: *"The Bible is the greatest of all books; to study it is the noblest of all pursuits; to understand it, the highest of all goals."* His words are worth writing out and placing in a prominent place above one's desk. Bible study should be exciting. To many, however, its message seems to be "sealed" (cf. Daniel 8:26, AV) and they lack the necessary knowledge and skill to unlock its treasures.

Certain basic reference tools can make all the difference in the world to the would-be Bible student. These include the use of:

- A Bible atlas
- A Bible concordance
- Bible commentaries.

Each of these resources will contribute toward a foundation upon which to build a solid, biblically oriented approach to life.

Bible Atlases

Bible atlases are available in almost every bookstore. It seems as if each publishing house has its own. And their nature and variety is sufficient to boggle the mind of the researcher. Evaluations of different atlases have been provided in *The Minister's Library*. In this chapter we will limit ourselves to only three of the many Bible atlases available today:

The Zondervan NIV Atlas of the Bible

The Macmillan Bible Atlas

The Moody Atlas of the Bible

As far as personal Bible study is concerned, the maps in a Bible atlas—though limited— should be sufficiently detailed to accurately plot historic sites, give the names as they appeared in biblical times, and show ancient roads and highways and places of importance. Geographical features should also be clearly marked, but not so as to crowd the text on a given page. And longitude and latitude should show the location of places in terms of degrees from the Equator and the Prime Meridian.

The *Zondervan NIV Atlas of the Bible* by Carl G. Rasmussen (1989) is a work with many excellent features. Replete with colorful maps by Carta of Jerusalem, the reader soon becomes aware of the fact that this work is in reality an historical geography of the lands of the Bible. This does not detract from its value, but only serves to warn the beginning Bible student that not everything with the word "atlas" in the title is in reality an atlas.

The biblical text used throughout this atlas is the New International Version (NIV), but this does little to improve the overall worth of this work. The value of what Rasmussen wrote lies in his eye-witness report of the geographic features of the Holy Land coupled with a masterful description of different historic events that took place at these sites. The result is an "atlas" that lends itself to being read through from cover to cover. Used in this way, the benefit to the user will be great.

The *Macmillan Bible Atlas* was edited by Y. Aharoni and M. Avi-Yonah—two Jewish scholars of international repute. The revised third edition (1993) is the work of A. F. Rainey and Z. Safrai. *MBA* is a work of rare excellence, containing maps identifying biblical sites and events; and inasmuch as it follows the chronology of the Bible (though some of the dating is questionable), it may be used to good effect whenever one is studying an historical book of either the Old or New Testament. Concentration is on the Holy Land, and so it evidences a lack when it comes to treating the expansion of the early Church. In spite of this limitation, *MBA* quickly grows on the user until it becomes one of the first sources (if not *the* first) the researcher reaches for whenever trying to locate where an event took place.

The *Moody Atlas of the Bible* by Barry J. Beitzel (1985) is a work of considerable erudition. It begins appropriately with an extensive section on "The Physical Geography of the Holy Land," and this is followed by informative discussions of "The Historical Geography of the Holy Land" and "The History of Biblical Mapmaking." Colored maps, plates and pictures further enhance this excellent work. Coverage extends to both Testaments, the Old as well as the New.

By means of an atlas you will be able to locate as nearly as possible the *places* made famous by those living in Bible times (e.g., Shechem, Bethel, Shiloh, Mizpah, Zion, Ephesus, Troas [ancient Troy], Athens, Corinth, Rome, and the islands of the Mediterranean visited by the Apostle Paul during his travels), and trace the *movements* of peoples and armies (e.g., the route of the Exodus, the settlement of the twelve tribes in Canaan, and attacks upon Jerusalem by Syrians, Assyrians, Babylonians, Egyptians, Romans). And you will also come to understand the significance of *events* mentioned in the Bible (e.g., the routing of Sisera's army, Judges chap. 4; the location of Joppa, Tarshish and Nineveh in the Book of Jonah; the close proximity of Bethpage and Bethany to the Mount of Olives, Luke 19:29), and a host of other details.

A second valuable resource tool to aid you in your study is a concordance to the Bible.

Bible Concordances

There are concordances to virtually every Bible translation or version: e.g., the Authorized Version (abbreviated AV, and also called the King James Version), Revised Standard Version (RSV) and the New Revised Standard Version (NRSV), the *New Living Translation*, the *New International Version* (NIV), the New American Standard Bible (NASB), and the New English Bible (NEB)—to name only a few. For an explanation of the strengths and weaknesses of these Bibles, see *The Minister's Library*.

Most people use a concordance when they are trying to locate a verse in the Bible. A concordance, however, has many other uses. It can be used to:

- Ascertain the usage of a word (e.g., "compassion," "constrain") because it is the usage of the word that determines its meaning

- Learn the different shades of meaning of a word--nuances which are not apparent from the reading of the English text (e.g., Paul's twofold use of "another" in Galatians 1:6-7, the former implying another of the same kind, and the latter insisting on their belief being another of a different kind)

- Trace a biblical writer's emphasis (e.g., Paul's use of "law" in Galatians; the emphasis on "Spirit" in Romans 8; the conflict between "light" and "darkness" and "belief" and "unbelief" in John's Gospel, and his first epistle)

- Observe the growth of an idea or doctrine in the Old and New Testaments (e.g., the development of sacrificial worship, the typology of the Tabernacle, the rise of the monarchy--all of which prefigure truths developed as the Scriptures unfold. Some of these truths may point to Christ's person and work. Such usage follows closely God's progressive revelation)

• Highlight references to places invested with importance in the Bible due to events which transpired in, on, or near them (e.g., Jacob's vow at Bethel; the Israelites frequent return to Gilgal; the Valley of Achor becoming a "door of hope"; Bethany being the town of Mary and Martha; the destruction of the temple at Shiloh, etc.)

• Develop a distinctively biblical theology through the study of specific words (e.g., reconciliation, redemption, resurrection, revelation, and much more), or Christ's claim to be the "Son of Man" (which some have thought is a term referring to His humanity while the expression "Son of God" has to do with His deity. From a study of *all* the passages in which this expression is used, we are led to conclude that "Son of Man" is a Messianic term implying royalty, for Daniel speaks of His "everlasting dominion" and that "all the peoples, nations, and languages shall serve Him" [Daniel 7:27]).

As a diligent Bible student, therefore, you will want to be like the "scribe" of Matthew 13:52 who, having become a "disciple of the kingdom of heaven" is like a householder who brings forth out of his "treasure" (i.e., your knowledge of Scripture) things new and old. That being the case, how will concordances help you achieve this goal; and what concordances are deserving of your consideration?

One word of caution: *Avoid using an abridged concordance.* You will in all likelihood become frustrated, and this may lead to some discouragement. So choose an *un*abridged work.

So which concordance should you use?

First, you will probably wish to consult a concordance that is based on the translation of the Bible you are presently using (e.g., NIV, NASB, NKJV). In one way or another all modern concordances owe a debt to the past, and it is helpful to have an understanding of the leading works of the recent past so as to be aware of the strengths upon which contemporary compilers have relied. Take, for example, the *Analytical Concordance to the Bible* by Robert Young (1879/1955), and the *Exhaustive Concordance of the Bible* by James Strong (1890/1965). Comparatively recent concordances owe much to the labors of Drs. Young and Strong; and the *New King James Exhaustive Concordance* (1992), and the *New American Standard Exhaustive Concordance of the Bible* (1981), and the *New International Version Exhaustive Concordance* (by E. W.Goodrich and John R. Kohlenberger III, 1990) have been patterned after them.

In describing the essential features of those concordances that have either stood the test of time or will most likely be of significant help to you, we shall begin with Robert Young's *Analytical Concordance to the Bible*. It is based on the text of the AV and the form of the different Greek and Hebrew words accompany the English word. "Young's" also provides ready reference to each passage in which that word appears, making it easy to study words like "faith," "love," and "obedience." The arrangement also shows how different Hebrew and Greek words have been translated by a single English word (e.g., "lord," "sleep," "son," "will"). The flexibility as well as the precision of the original languages is thus readily evident. Included at the end of Young's *Analytical Concordance* is a handy lexicon to words appearing in the Old and New Testaments.

Of a different nature is James Strong's *Exhaustive Concordance of the Bible*. Like "Young's" it has gone through many printings, one of the most recent being 1990. It, too, is based on the AV (as is the *New Strong's Exhaustive Concordance*), and the format established by Strong has set a standard of excellence for accuracy and completeness.

A unique feature of Strong's *Concordance* is the fact that against each entry there is a number directing the researcher to a Hebrew or Greek index at the back that contains information about the word used and its meaning(s). For example, under "offering" a number is indicated: 4503. Lower down, another number is given: 8641. References to 4503 and 8641 in the "Hebrew and Chaldee Dictionary" at the back will give you the meaning(s) of each word. And Greek words can be traced in the same way. What this means is that with little technical knowledge of the biblical languages, you may have access to the learning of others. And the *Theological Wordbook of the Old Testament* and the Logos Library System on CD-ROM (to name only two of many reference sources) have been coded to Strong's *Concordance*.

Patterned after Strong's *Concordance*, and illustrative of the new works available today, is the *New American Standard Exhaustive Concordance of the Bible*, edited by R. L. Thomas (1981). It lists every word which may be used to locate a verse in the NASB and also notes the Hebrew, Aramaic or Greek word from which the English word is translated. More than ten years of painstaking effort went into the preparation of this volume and computers were used to compile an alphabetical listing of all English words and their frequency. More than 400,000 entries make up this handy resource tool.

As with Strong's *Concordance*, the Hebrew-Aramaic and Greek dictionaries included at the back of the *NASB Concordance* are particularly helpful. They have been arranged in such a way that those lacking a knowledge of the original languages may nevertheless be appraised of the root form of the word, the frequency of its occurrence, and its meaning(s). All things considered, the *NASB Concordance* is a most valuable reference work.

Having learned how to research biblical information for yourself through the use of Bible atlases and concordances, you are now in a position to investigate the viewpoints of others.[12]

Bible Commentaries

So many sets of commentaries on the Scriptures have been published that it is hard to isolate the ones with which you should be familiar. If you are in any doubt as to the reliability of a work, reference can always be made to *The Minister's Library*. This is especially true when you desire to have information about works not treated in this chapter. In time, however, you will probably come to prefer individual treatments of the books of the Bible like W. H. Griffith Thomas' *Genesis*, S. H. Kellogg's *Leviticus*, Leon Morris' *The Gospel According to John,* John R. W. Stott's *God's New Society* (Ephesians), and Ray C. Stedman's *Expository Studies in 1 John.*

For our purposes we will concentrate on the following multivolume sets:

The Anchor Bible

The Expositor's Bible

The Expositor's Bible Commentary

The International Critical Commentary

Interpreter's Bible

The New Interpreter's Bible

Keil and Delitzsch's *Biblical Commentary on the Old Testament*

Lenski's *The Interpretation of the New Testament*

The New International Commentary on the New Testament

The New International Commentary on the Old Testament

The New International Greek Testament Commentary

The Tyndale New Testament Commentaries

The Tyndale Old Testament Commentaries

The Anchor Bible, edited by W. F. Albright and D. N. Freedman (1964-present), when completed, will include the canonical books of both testaments and the Apocrypha. The philological scholarship undergirding these commentaries is unquestioned. The contributors have been drawn from Protestant, Catholic and Jewish backgrounds. While the purpose behind the publication of *The Anchor Bible* is to make available to the general reader the benefits of modern biblical scholarship, some of the commentaries contributed to this series are highly technical and are better suited to the needs of the theologian or the aspiring theologue. Helpful documentation precedes each section, and those with a solid background in the Scriptures will appreciate the excellent contributions of E. A. Speiser (*Genesis*), M. Dahood (*Psalms*), J. Bright (*Jeremiah*), F. I. Andersen (*Hosea*), R. Brown (*John's Gospel*), and M. Barth (*Ephesians*)— even though the theological perspective of many of these authors is neither evangelical nor conservative.

The Expositor's Bible, edited by W. R. Nicoll, was originally published in England between 1887-1896 (in 49 volumes). It is a valuable work and contains some of the finest expository studies ever published (e.g., Blaikie on *Joshua* and *I and II Samuel*, Maclaren on the *Psalms* (3 vols.), *Colossians* and *Philemon*, and Moule on *Romans*). Not all the treatments are of equal merit, however, for Samuel Cox's handling of Ecclesiastes, though it is of great value, denies its Solomonic authorship.

Some of the more liberal treatments in *The Expositor's Bible* are to be found in Farrar's treatment of *First and Second Kings*, Bennett's handling of the *Books of Chronicles* (an excellent work which has unfortunately been marred by his dogmatic adherence to theories about the sources of the text), and Sir George Adam Smith's expositions of *Jeremiah* and *The Book of the Twelve Prophets*—both of which earned him considerable renown.

The Expositor's Bible Commentary, edited by F. E. Gaebelein (12 vols., 1976-92), is based on the text of the NIV. At times this necessitates that an author spend as much space correcting the text as he does expounding it. Volume 1 contains introductory articles covering a variety of biblical and theological themes. These are of significant value. Volumes 2 through 12 contain expositions of the books of the Bible. Some are praiseworthy (e.g., Exodus, Matthew, Thessalonian Epistles), but the majority *(though written by capable scholars!)* lack significance because inadequate space was allocated by the editor, and they are therefore too brief to be worthy of a student's time.

The International Critical Commentary on the Holy Scriptures of the Old and New Testaments, edited by S. R. Driver, A. Plummer and C. A. Briggs (Incomplete; 1895-1951) deserves consultation, for some of the volumes are of outstanding value. And this is in spite of the fact that the *ICC* has consistently maintained a theologically liberal standard of scholarship. However, Plummer on *Luke* and *II Corinthians*, Bernard on *John's Gospel,* Sanday and Headlam on *Romans*, Robertson and Plummer on *I Corinthians*, and Burton on *Galatians*, established a mark of exegetical, philological, historical and textual competence that is hard to equal.

A new edition of the *ICC*, under the editorial guidance of J. A. Emerton (Old Testament) and C. E. B. Cranfield (New Testament), was begun in 1975 with the first of Cranfield's volumes on *Romans*. This was a pace-setting work, and, like its predecessors, demands the attention of students of the Bible. Since then other exegetical books have appeared, notably McKane on *Jeremiah*, Davis and Allison on *Matthew*, Barrett on *Acts*, and Margaret Thrall on *Second Corinthians*.

The *Interpreter's Bible*, edited by G. A. Buttrick et al (12 vols.; 1951-1957), uses the text of the AV and RSV, and aims at being both exegetical and expository. Volume I contains articles pertaining to the inspiration, canonicity, texts, history of transmission, et cetera, of the Bible. Comments on each canonical book follow and are treated in the order in which they appear in our English Bibles. Though designed for the general reader and preacher, negative theories about the authorship, as well as the sources and transmission and reliability of the text abound, and this reduces the value of this set. In the years since the appearance of *IB*, many of the left-wing views espoused by the contributors have beendiscarded (sometimes even by those scholars who at one time held to them), because archaeological evidence has proved the unity of a particular book or shown that the normal meaning of the text is the right one. This has called for a revision of the entire work.

The New Interpreter's Bible (1994-) is now in process. It is scheduled for 12 volumes and the volumes available thus far use the text of the NRSV and NIV in parallel columns. The early volumes in this series appear on the surface to be less critical of the biblical text than their predecessors, but this irenic impression soon fades when one takes note of the adherence of the contributors to form- and redaction-criticism, and other approaches to matters of interpretation that leave the neophyte at the mercy of the scholar. The Apocryphal volumes are of interest historically and linguistically, but they should never be granted parity with the canonical books of the Bible.

The *Biblical Commentary on the Old Testament*, by C. F. Keil and F. J. Delitzsch (25 vols.; 1956), was produced by two evangelical German scholars during the latter part of the nineteenth century. Issues involving the grammar and syntax of the text are dealt with impartially and with such a lack of ostentation that readers are inclined to treat lightly the contribution of these devout men of God. Problems in interpretation are not glossed over. In fact, these are treated in a very candid manner and a plausible solution is offered to the reader. At times the authors hold to a moderate documentary hypothesis, but in general this is not allowed to interfere with their exposition of the text. While modern researchers may be inclined to dismiss "K and D" (sometimes cited as KD) because recent philological and archaeological investigations have elucidated what was formerly obscure, the fact remains that these diligent expositors produced a work which has placed the entire Christian world in their debt.

The Interpretation of the New Testament, by R. C. H. Lenski (14 vols.; 1934-1966), is based on Lenski's own recession of the Greek manuscripts and does not always agree with either the Nestle text or the Textus Receptus. Each volume, however, bears mute testimony to its author's painstaking labors. Historical details are carefully blended with perceptive comments on the text, and critical problems are handled in a judicious manner. In spite of Lenski's rigidity in treating certain Greek tenses, his commentaries are deserving of careful consideration. It will be only on rare occasions that a student will arise from a careful study of one of these books without having had his/her heart blessed and his/her thinking stretched by this capable Lutheran expositor.

The New International Commentary on the New Testament (1951-present) began under the editorship of Ned B. Stonehouse. Upon his death the editorial "mantle" fell on the shoulders of F. F. Bruce. Now it has devolved upon Gordon Fee, who is supervising the revision of certain studies and commissioning the writing of others.

The expositions are generally representative of the best of modern Reformed scholarship, and this work has taken its place among those most serviceable to the busy pastor and the more advanced Bible student. Though using different English texts (e.g., American Standard Version, 1901) as the basis of an expository study, each contributor has to all intents and purposes based his treatment of the text on his own translation. Technical matters have been confined to the footnotes. Elaboration on important issues, grammatical and textual factors highlighting some facet of the teaching of God's Word, and historical details, will be found in special notes in the appendixes.

The contributors to this series have been drawn from many lands. Of particular significance to the researcher will be Lane's work on *Mark*, Morris' treatment of *John's Gospel*, Bruce's expositions of *Acts* and *Hebrews*, Hughes' magisterial handling of *II Corinthians*, and Marshall's explanation of *John's Epistles*.

The New International Commentary on the Old Testament (1976-present) was originally launched under the editorship of the late E. J. Young (who contributed the first three volumes to the series on the *Book of Isaiah*). Upon his death the task of bringing the work to completion fell to R. K. Harrison. This series, like its New Testament counter-part, is representative of the best of modern, evangelical Reformed schol-arship. Each book is carefully introduced and this is generally followed by an elucidating exposition. Documentation is reserved for the foot-notes. Extensive use is made of data from archaeological "digs," and philological comparisons are made from the Masoretic text to informa-tion gleaned from the Dead Sea Scrolls, the LXX, or other Near Eastern languages.

While varying in quality and reliability, the volumes produced thus far have added a new dimension to the study of the Old Testament.

The New International Greek Testament Commentary (1978-present) is being edited by I. Howard Marshall and W. Ward Gasque. So far half a dozen volumes have appeared. All reveal the hand of the scholar, deal-ing deftly with the nuances of the original in an effort to accurately un-derstand the message of the New Testament and, in this way, aid the pas-tor and seminary student in his or her understanding of the text. It is to be regretted that modern criticism played a major role in Marshall's schol-arly study of *Luke's Gospel,* so much so that greater effort was spent trying to identify the sources of "Q" than in explaining the meaning of the text to his readers.

The Tyndale New Testament Commentaries, formerly edited by R. V. G. Tasker, are now under the editorship of L. L. Morris (20 vols.; 1957-1974). The series is designed for lay people. The volumes are not overly technical; each work is the product of a fine evangelical scholar who has brought to his exposition of the text a background rich in Greek literature and exegesis; and the result is a series that is brief, informative and practical.

Initially the commentaries were all based on the AV, but toward the end of the original series, and in the revised volumes, each writer has been given the liberty to use the English text of his choice, and provide his own translation.

Outstanding contributions to the original series included Cole on *Mark,* Morris on *Luke,* Bruce on *Romans*, Foulkes on *Ephesians,* Guthrie on *The Pastoral Epistles*, Green on *II Peter and Jude*, and Stott on *John's Epistles.* With the passing of time certain volumes have been "retired" and others works have been revised (though so far most of the revision-ary work is to be found in the Introduction to each book with very little change in the exposition).

The Tyndale Old Testament Commentaries, edited by D. J. Wiseman (1974-present), is aimed at providing lay people with a handy, up-to-date commentary on each book of the Old Testament. The series has already distinguished itself for its blending of extra-biblical information (history, archaeology, philology) with an explanation of the meaning of the text. Major critical questions are discussed in the introduction to each canonical book, and additional notes are included where needed. Cole's handling of *Exodus* evidences much wisdom in condensing all that might have been said into a succinct commentary. Unfortunately his dating of the Exodus and the route taken by the Israelites leaves too many questions unanswered. Thompson's *Deuteronomy* is excellent; Harrison's *Jeremiah/Lamentations* and more recently *Leviticus* are deserving of the highest praise; Morris on *Ruth* is well done; and Kidner's *Ezra/Nehemiah, Psalms* (2 vols.) and *Proverbs* contain a wealth of information. Some volumes, however (e.g., *Judges* and *I and II Samuel*) make too many concessions to those who look for evidence of different redactors and this can be disconcerting to the reader.

This series bears watching, particularly as new volumes are added at regular intervals.

In this chapter we have looked briefly at Bible atlases, Bible concordances, and Bible commentaries. All of these resource tools can enrich your study of the Word of God. In our next chapter we will seek to assess the value of lexical aids (i.e., Greek and Hebrew concordances) which can assist you understand with greater precision the meaning of Hebrew and Greek words.

LOOKING AHEAD

Webster defined a concordance as an "alphabetical index to the principal words of a book, as of the Bible, with a reference to the passage in which each occurs and some part of the context." One of the uses of a concordance is that it facilitates the tracing of different words so that they can be studied in context.

By checking the entries in Young's *Analytical Concordance to the Bible* listing words for "anger," "child," and "everlasting," identify both the Hebrew and Greek terms. Compare the entries found in Young's *Concordance* with those listed in the *Englishman's Hebrew and Chaldee Concordance* and the *Englishman's Greek Concordance to the New Testament.* More advanced students should use Mandelkern's *Veteris testamenti concordantiae Habraicae atque Chaldaicae* and Moulton and Geden's *Concordance to the Greek Testament.*

How well does each reference work cover the usage of the word? What is the value of these works as resource tools? How would you go about analyzing and then summarizing the biblical data?

In recalling the student mentioned in chapter 1 who had been assigned the task of researching the usage and meaning of the word *apostasia,* and by using a combination of the resources mentioned above, list those passages in the Bible where this word is used together with its possible meaning(s). To what extent is the context of help to you in determining the meaning?

6

The Use of Concordances

Have you ever wondered how a person such as William Barclay could find so many interesting and informative things to say about different words or terms used to describe people, places or things in the Bible? He explained the secret in his Preface to *More New Testament Words*:

> The more I study words, the more I am convinced of their basic and fundamental importance. On the meaning of words everything depends. No one can build up a theology without a clear definition of the terms that are to be used in it. No one can construct a Christian ethic without a close study of the great ethical terms of the New Testament. Christian belief and Christian action both depend upon a clear understanding of the meaning of words.[13]

In the same vein, when was the last time you saw someone really become excited over something which he or she had discovered as a result of his or her study of the Scriptures? Why is it that the things taught us from the pulpit frequently reflect a monotonous sameness that eventually deteriorates into a dry, pedantic rehearsal of the old, the familiar, and the bland?

A faculty member who is well known to us was asked to teach a two-semester course in Biblical Studies to a class of freshmen psychology students. Each semester he assigned them the task of writing on a Bible character of their choice. In the Fall they would write on someone from the Old Testament, and in the Spring they would write on someone from the New.

As each student began researching his or her Bible character, they sooner or later came to the point of considering descriptive phrases or statements made about the person of their choice. Rebekah, for example, is described with purposeful repetition as "a virgin" with whom no man had sexual relations (Genesis 24:16). The significance of this may be traced to the culture of the people and the morality of the times. Of King Jehoram of Judah we read that when he died, "He departed with no one's regret" (2 Chronicles 21:20). In the New Testament, the ascended Christ specifically praised Antipas for his faithfulness to the truth, even in the face of persecution that resulted in martyrdom (Revelation 2:13). And David had his entire life summarized by the word "servant" (Acts 13:36; see also 2 Samuel 24:17).

The better one knows the Bible, the easier it is to find other illustrations of this principle.

One Spring a young man came to us obviously bubbling over with excitement. In studying Nathanael he had been prompted to dig into some concordances and lexicons in order to trace the etymology of the word "guile" (John 1:47). He had had no previous training in Greek and the task was a difficult one. Imagine his delight when he found that "guile" originally had been a word used to describe the bait a fisherman would put on a hook. It was the promise of food that caused an unsuspecting fish to take the hook. In time, this same word came to be applied to people--con artists, we would call them today--who deceived others. Appropriately, they were observed to "bait" people into falling into their trap. They came to be looked upon as being full of guile.

Word studies can be exciting. Their value can readily be seen in a book like William Barclay's *Flesh and Spirit* (1962) in which he expounds the terms used by the Apostle Paul in Galatians 5:19-23. And Donald Grey Barnhouse, for thirty-three years pastor of the historic Tenth Presbyterian Church, Philadelphia, told of his own practice of studying the Scriptures. He traveled a great deal and always took with him suitcases containing Greek and Hebrew texts of the Bible and about 22 concordances and lexicons. As he studied a passage, he would trace the meaning of significant words throughout the entire Bible. Then, as he expounded the text, he would illustrate the meaning of a word from Genesis through Revelation. His *Exposition of Bible Doctrine* (10 vols.; 1952-1963) on Paul's letter to the church in Rome is illustrative of his approach.

Our initial interest lies in specific terms used in Scripture. Some of these are already well known to us (e.g., justification, propitiation, sanctification). Illustrations of theological word studies done on these terms may be found in Leon Morris' *The Apostolic Preaching of the Cross* (1955). Our concern here is with the methodology by which accurate ideas of words and their meaning(s) may be obtained. Chapters 8 and 9 will build upon this chapter and deal specifically with the process of doing word studies.

When we consider the resource tools available for biblical research, they divide into two obvious groups: Those dealing with the text of the Old Testament, and those dealing with the text of the New. The former can be expected to focus on the meaning of Hebrew and Aramaic words, and the latter on the terms and expressions commonly used at the time of Christ and the Apostles.

An additional resource is the Septuagint (LXX)--the translation of the Old Testament into Greek.

Old Testament Resources

While students who lack an understanding of Hebrew will find Young's *Analytical Concordance to the Bible* invaluable, they should also become familiar with the work edited by George V. Wigram, *The Englishman's Hebrew and Chaldee Concordance of the Old Testament* (5th. ed.; 1890). Arranged by Hebrew word, this concordance lists passages in the Old Testament containing the term with its translation in the Authorized (or King James) Version.

Because it is the usage of the word that determines its meaning, and because language is constantly changing, by using a concordance you will be able to (1) assess the general meaning of a given word, and (2) tie in its usage with different writers and/or eras of history (e.g., Mosaic period, united or divided monarchy, early or later prophets).

Two other concordances dealing with the Old Testament are indispensable to its study. These are:

Mandelkern's *Veteris testamenti concordantiae Habraicae atque Chaldaicae*, and

Lisowsky's *Konkordanz zum hebraischen Alten Testament.*

Students who have not yet taken courses in the original languages of the Bible may at first be intimidated by the titles of these two works. Don't be! As you begin to use them your fear will gradually disappear.

Solomon Mandelkern's *Veteris testamenti concordantiae Habraicae atque Chaldaicae* (1955) contains citations according to sense, proper placement of entries misplaced under false roots, correction of grammatical confusions, and the addition of *hapax legomena* omitted in previous works. Even if the beginning student does little more than use the biblical references listed at the side of each citation, his or her study of Scripture will be immeasurably enhanced due to the accuracy of this important resource. For the more advanced student, Mandelkern's now famous concordance will not only give the accuracy that thorough research requires, but will also enable him or her to study words in relationship to important grammatical distinctions.

Of similar value is Gerhard Lisowsky's *Konkordanz zum hebraischen Alten Testament* (1958), which has been photographically reproduced from Lisowsky's handwritten manuscript. With emphasis placed on nouns and verbs, this concordance is particularly helpful to the student engaged in word studies.

Of course, with the translation in the second century B.C. of the Old Testament into Greek, the zealous student will wish to compare the Greek words used to translate their Hebrew equivalent. A valuable reference work in this area is the *Concordance to the Septuagint... (including the Apocryphal Books)* by Edwin Hatch and Henry Redpath (3 vols. in 2; 1892-1906/1987). Each Greek word in the canonical and apocryphal books is listed with its Hebrew counterpart in a corresponding numerical sequence. Because the usage of a given word is crucial in determining its meaning(s), the inclusion in this instance of the Apocrypha is fortuitous. Were this not the case, we would have had to seek for another concordance that would alert us to word usage in these ancient, non-canonical writings.

New Testament Resources

Concordances to the New Testament, particularly in German, are legion. For this reason it is important for us to confine ourselves to only a few. Regardless of your knowledge of Greek, you should find at least one of the following helpful.

The Englishman's Greek Concordance to the New Testament

Moulton and Geden's *Concordance to the Greek Testament*

Computer concordance to the Novum Testamentum Graece.

G. K. Gillespie's *Englishman's Greek Concordance to the New Testament* (9th ed., edited by George V. Wigram; 1903/1976) is arranged in the same way as its Old Testament counterpart. It is based on the text of the AV and cites in alphabetical order by the Greek word the Biblical references together with a brief quotation. It is relatively easy, therefore, to determine the meaning(s) assigned a word by the translators of the Authorized (King James) Version of the Bible. Included in this monumental tome is a complete index of the words of the English text with the Greek words from which they are translated. From this index the student will find, for example, a listing of the twenty-seven different English words used to translate *logos* ("word").

The *Concordance to the Greek Testament* by William F. Moulton and Albert S. Geden (1897, revised by H. K. Moulton in 1978, and reprinted in 1986), is now complete with full citations including particles like *apo, en, hoti*, and *sun*. As such it has become one of the basic reference tools for students of the New Testament. Familiarly known as "Moulton and Geden," it is based upon the text of Westcott and Hort. Users will find that it contains quotations of Scripture that are longer than in most concordances of its kind. It is replete with grammatical hints, the usage of the word in the LXX and Apocrypha, and citations in Hebrew (if the passage in question happens to be a quotation from the Old Testament).

The valuable *Computer concordance to the Novum Testamentum Graece/Computer-Konkordanz zum Novum Testamentum Graece* (2d ed., 1985) is indispensable to the study of specific Greek words used in the New Testament. Based upon the 26th edition of the Nestle-Aland text and the 3rd edition of the United Bible Societies' *Greek New Testament*, this beautifully produced concordance lists every word appearing in the New Testament with the frequency of its occurrence. Each quotation is lengthy, and this enables the researcher to better assess the context in which the word appears.

As a general rule, words are arranged in accordance with their root form. In the case of some irregular verbs, however, the word is also listed under the different forms. Words occurring in pericope are included with an asterisk following each entry. An appendix lists the appearance of conjunctions, particles, et cetera.

LOOKING AHEAD

In preparation for a further discussion of words and their meaning, take special note (1) of the way in which *hesed*, "lovingkindness," is treated in the *Theological Wordbook of the Old Testament* by R. L. Harris, G. L. Archer and B. K. Waltke; and (2) study carefully the article on "discipleship" in the *New International Dictionary of New Testament Theology*, edited by Colin Brown. Check on the sequence of thought, the sources from which the information is gleaned, and the movement from one historic period to the next.

7

The Importance of Lexicons

Whereas concordances provide us with an alphabetical index of the principal words of a book (e.g., the Bible) or a writer (e.g., Moses, Paul), and a reference to the passage in which each mention of a word occurs (e.g., "transgression," in Hebrews 2:2) together with some indication of the context, a lexicon may be described as a "wordbook or dictionary of a specific language, or the vocabulary of a particular people." A lexicon is compiled to describe in succinct terms the meaning(s) of a given word. The etymology is traced through the successive stages of the history of the language.

HEBREW LEXICONS

Early History

Hebrew lexicography dates back to the 9th century A.D. Like all pioneer efforts, these early lexicons laid a foundation upon which later works were built. It was not until the time of Wilhelm Gesenius (1786-1842) that the first modern dictionary was produced under the title *Hebraisches-deutsches Handworterbuch uber die Schriften des Alten Testaments* (2 vols.; 1810-1812).

It was natural for those living in a day when scholars read and spoke several different languages to give their works impressive titles in French or German ... or Latin. Don't let these titles intimidate you. In a very short time you'll get used to them!

Gesenius' work has stood the test of time. After seventeen editions, and under the general editorship of Frantz Buhl, it reappeared bearing the title *Hebraisches und aramaisches Handworterbuch uber das Alte Testament* (1922). But we are moving ahead of ourselves. While Gesenius was still alive a companion volume to his Hebrew handbook began to be published. It was completed posthumously, and was called the *Thesarus philologicus-criticus linguae Hebraeae et Chaldaeae Veteris Testament*

(1829-1858). This philological lexicon serves as a monument to Gesenius' tireless industry and thoroughness, as well as his extensive knowledge of Hebrew and other cognate languages. Its value to us lies in the fact that three British scholars: F. Brown, S. R. Driver and C. A. Briggs, translated and edited it, and published their revision under the title *A Hebrew and English Lexicon of the Old Testament.* (This work is often referred to as "BDB," and more will be said about it later on in this chapter.)

Other important lexicographical works followed the publication of Gesenius' dictionary in 1810. It was not until 1876, however, that a comprehensive lexicon appeared dealing with the post-Biblical Hebrew and Aramaic era. Jacob Levy's *Neuhebraisches und chaldaisches worterbuch uber die Talmudim und Midraschim* (1876-1889; 2d ed., 1924) and his *Chaldaisches Worterbuch uber die Targumim* (1881) provided access to the Talmudic and Midrashic literature of the Jews. These works bore some resemblance to Johann Buxtorf's *Lexicon Chaldaicum, Talmidicum et Rabbinicum* (1639) and Edmund Castell's *Lexicon Heptaglotton Hebraicum, Chaldaicum, Syriacum, Samaritanum, Aethiopicum, Arabicum et Persicum* (1669), but were more complete.

Now, of course, translations of the Talmud, Midrash and Mishnah are available in English, so the student doesn't have to read them in Hebrew. It is still necessary, however, for researchers to use these old works when tracing the usage of particular word.

Modern Resources

BDB first appeared in 1907, and was last revised in 1962. It depended heavily on comparative linguistics and readily translated similar terms in a variety of Near Eastern languages. The value of BDB lies in the fact that the editors were sensitive to the nuances or shades of meaning of Classical Hebrew, and this gave their work an enduring quality that is not to be found in other, more recent, lexicons that lack flexibility when assigning specific meanings to words.

One of the works that never attained the stature of BDB was the *Lexicon in Veteris Testamenti Libros*, edited by L. Koehler and W. Baumgartner (2 vols.; 1951-1953). It provided a Hebrew/Aramaic German/English explanation of words and their meanings and was based on the third edition of Rudolf Kittel's *Biblia Hebraica.* The order of the words in this lexicon is strictly alphabetical and not by root as in BDB. Usage is also made of Ugaritic sources not available to BDB.

Koehler and Baumgartner's *Lexicon* has now been revised by Baumgartner and J. J. Stamm, and is in the process of being translated and edited by M. E. J. Richardson (1994-). The new edition is being issued under the title *Hebrew and Aramaic Lexicon of the Old Testament*. So far, four out of five promised volumes have been published. This revision makes full use of Ugaritic materials and information from the Dead Sea Scrolls. A feature that makes this new edition more usable to students of Biblical Hebrew is the fact that words from other cognate languages are transliterated. Only Hebrew and Greek words are written in their own alphabets.

As far as can be ascertained, this new edition of K-B has special value in the area of etymological research and in tracing *hapax legomena*. Though the meanings assigned different words are often influenced by critical considerations, the conclusions offered can always be checked against BDB. Advanced students will find valuable information in the bibliography.

Also in process at the present time is the *Dictionary of Classical Hebrew*, edited by D. J. A. Clines (1993-). Scheduled for eight volumes, this lexicon is in many respects the first entirely new work to be published in many years. Other lexicons such as BDB and the new K-B were based upon earlier works. Clines' *DCH* follows a strictly alphabetical order for the entries as they appear in sentences (as opposed to BDB where words were placed under the tri-lateral root). No cognates from other Semitic languages are mentioned, but inscriptional evidence down to A.D. 200, together with data from Qumran and Ben Sira, has been included. As a result, this dictionary does not provide information about connections with other Semitic dialects and it does not classify usages as figurative or literal. Related words, synonyms, and antonyms are listed at the end of the treatment of a word. Emendations proposed by BDB and K-B are listed, but without any critical evaluation.

DCH gives promise of being a valuable tool for the scholar. Its strength lies in its semantic examination of each word, syntagmatic listing of every usage with its meaning, and paradigmatic listing of synonyms and antonyms. It concludes with an English-Hebrew index, and an English translation of every Hebrew word or phrase. Though *avant-garde* and highly commendable, its projected size and cost will place it beyond the reach of the average student of the biblical languages. It is unlikely, therefore, to replace BDB for practical usefulness.

By means of a lexicon, you, as an eager and inquiring researcher, will be able to verify speedily and easily the results of your investigation of Hebrew words and their meaning *via* the numerous concordances. It now remains for us to consider Greek works paralleling those Hebrew resources.

GREEK LEXICONS

The history of Greek literature has been classified in different ways. For our purpose we will deal with the writings of the Greeks in five broad periods of time. Each of these five eras is capable of further subdivision. For convenience, however, we will look at the periods of literary development as follows:

- *The early period* (2nd millennium to c. 950 B.C.), consisting of hymns to the gods, harvest songs, war songs, dirges--all of which provided resource material for writers in the classical period.

- *The classical period* (c. 950 to 330 B.C.), which included the writings of Homer, Hesiod, Euripedes, Xenophon, Thuycidides, Aristophenes, Herodotus, Aristotle, Demosthenes, and many more.

- *The Hellenistic period* (330 B.C. to about 325 A.D.), during which the *lingua franca* of the people was essentially the same as the Koine Greek of the New Testament. This era included Plutarch, Philo, Josephus, Polybius, the writers of the New Testament, Clement, Origen, Irenaeus, and others.

- *The Byzantine period* (from about 325 A.D. to 1453)--a period which lies outside the realm of our discussion; and

- *The modern period* (1453-present).

Our interest will be primarily with the third (Hellenistic) period. However, because many of the words used by the writers of the New Testament have their roots in the classical period, information from these writers of antiquity provides fertile ground for lexicographical research.

The Classical Period

One of the most widely used resources providing access to the classical period of Greek literature is the unabridged edition of H. C. Liddell and R. Scott's *Greek-English Lexicon* (1897/1996). A revised and updated edition was prepared for publication by H. S. Jones with the assistance of R. McKenzie (1940), and a Supplement by E. A. Barber was issued in 1968.

An index to the Greek authors and their works is to be found in the introductory material to Liddell and Scott. This index provides a key to the abbreviations used in the body of the lexicon (e.g., **D.H.** is Dionysius of Halicarnassus; **J.** is Josephus, *Vita*; and **Plu**. *Galb* is Plutarch[us], Lives [Galba]; etc.).

The Greek citations in Liddell and Scott may appear intimidating at first glance until you realize that the volumes published in the famous *Loeb Classical Library* (issued simultaneously in England and the United

States), make available a fine translation of these Greek classics. The format of these books is such that the Greek text is on one page and, facing it, an English translation. This makes it easy for you to study the word in its context. References to words in these classics are by book, chapter, and paragraph, or, on some occasions, to book, chapter, and line.

While Liddell and Scott's *Lexicon* is of value primarily for the access it provides to the classical period, literature is also cited through to the sixth century A.D. This includes the Septuagint and Apocrypha. Obviously, the closer the reference is to the New Testament era, the greater will be its bearing on the meaning of the word in the language of the people who lived during the era of Christ and the Apostles. One note of caution: Do *not* buy an abridged edition of Liddell and Scott. An abridgement may be useful to students of classical Greek, but it is valueless when studying the New Testament.

The most exhaustive resource to Greek literature (though at the present time few institutions have access to it) is the *Thesaurus Linguae Graecae* or *TLG* produced by the University of California, Irvine. Available in CD-ROM, *TLG* is a full-text database from the time of Homer to the 10th century A.D. It can be accessed via several different software packages and can be searched for by word or by phrase, or by combinations of words. As such it is a unique research tool that classical scholars, philologists, and students of the New Testament have found to be indispensable. In all, the writings of 3,200 authors have been accessed, making it the most complete work of its kind ever produced.

An illustration of how usage of a particular word determines its meaning may be found in T. J. Conant's *The Meaning and Use of Baptizein* (1860/1977). In this book Conant, who was a remarkable philologist, traced all of the uses of *baptizein* ("to baptize") and showed researchers how different contexts called for changes in meaning.

The Hellenistic Period

The Hellenistic period of Greek literature witnessed (1) the translation of the Old Testament and the Apocrypha into Greek; (2) the penning of the canonical books of the New Testament; (3) the writings of Jews such as Philo of Alexandria and Josephus; (4) the flourishing of Greek as the *lingua franca* of the Egyptians (as is evidenced by archaeological discoveries there); and (5) the era of the early Church Fathers. Sources providing you with access to this data are many. Here are three:

Bauer's *Greek-English Lexicon of the New Testament*

Moulton and Milligan's *Vocabulary of the Greek Testament*

Lampe's *Patristic Greek Lexicon*

The history behind the production of Walter Bauer's *Greek-English Lexicon of the New Testament and Other Early Christian Literature* (translated and edited by W. F. Arndt and F. W. Gingrich [1957-1958], and revised and augmented by F. W. Gingrich and F. W. Danker [1979]) has been told by Danker in *Multipurpose Tools for Bible Study.* At one time referred to as "Arndt and Gingrich," Bauer's lexicon is based upon an extensive examination of Greek literature, including New Testament words still in use in Byzantine times. A vast amount of material was mastered and then reduced to succinct, descriptive statements defining the usage of each word and giving its meaning during different eras of Greek literary history. The true value of this lexicon can only be appreciated as one reads through the prefatory material, and particularly the introduction by Bauer.

Sufficient to say that the coverage is excellent, the meaning(s) given each word is judicious, grammatical hints are of the utmost importance, and the references to literature outside the New Testament has been well-chosen and is representative of the usage of the same word in other sources. You will find Bauer's lexicon indispensable—whether used in an academic setting, or for private study, or on the mission field.

A second source of philological illumination comes from papyri discovered in Egypt. The terminology found in these papyrus fragments, letters and ostraka, parallels the Greek of the New Testament. Much of it, therefore, may be used to add new insights into the meaning of words employed by the writers of the New Testament.

The *Worterbuch der griechischen Papyrusurkunden mit Einschluss der griechischen Inschriften, Aufschriften, Ostraka, Mumienschilder usw. aus Agypten*, by F. Preisigke and E. Kiessling (3 vols.; 1925-1931; supplement 2, 1967-1976), deals exclusively with the vocabulary of the papyri unearthed by archaeologists in Egypt. This work is now only available in larger libraries, and so a work of related importance by J. H. Moulton and G. Milligan entitled *Vocabulary of the Greek Testament, Illustrated from the Papyri and Other Non-literary Sources* (1929) becomes indispensable as you study the usage of words in Egypt during this period.

Moulton and Milligan's *Vocabulary* is based upon articles published as "lexical notes" in *The Expositor* (1908-1911), with Part I appearing in 1914 and Part II in 1915. Following Moulton's tragic death in 1917, Milligan carried on the work alone, finally finishing this important resource tool in 1929.

Within the pages of Moulton and Milligan (often cited as M-M) you will find numerous parallels to the terminology of the New Testament. Furthermore, investigation of the source material offered in the concise format of this volume will not only enrich your study but also provide numerous illustrations of word usage in the language of the people of the New Testament period.

Finally, the *Patristic Greek Lexicon*, edited by G. H. W. Lampe (1961), places you in touch with the writings of the early Church Fathers. This volume is based upon the material contained in Migne's *Patrologia Graeca*, and took more than half a century to bring to completion. Its object is to make available the theological and ecclesiastical vocabulary of the Greek Christian authors from Clement of Rome to Theodore of Stadium, so that researchers can trace easily and efficiently the development of Christian thought. Informative coverage, therefore, is given terms like *apostolos, episkopos, presbuteros,* et cetera.

The values of a lexicon such as this one by Lampe, are many. First, as far as the development of doctrine is concerned, we can trace by example as well as precept either the early church's adherence to "sound doctrine" or its departure from it. The reasons for the latter frequently parallel trends in our own time, for while we tend to be more sophisticated, human nature remains the same and the origin of our defection is merely clothed in more acceptable terms.

Second, in the course of history, changes in the usage of words and their meaning were inevitable. It is interesting to note that the term "disciple," used so extensively in the Gospels of one who had counted the cost of following Christ, in the era of the early church came to be applied to those whose manner of life would permit this term to be connected with their name. Often death by martyrdom was regarded as the criterion for calling a person a "disciple." Such usage was a far cry from the meaning given the word by Christ, but shows the trend of the church following the death of the apostles. Too often today's "fast food" exegetes diminish the meaning simply to "learner."

In keeping with the format adopted by Liddell and Scott in their *Greek-English Lexicon*, this work by Lampe also begins with a list of the authors and their writings (e.g., **Iren**. *haer* is the abbreviation for Irenaeus Lugdunensis, *Adversus Haereses* ["Against Heresies"]; **Tat**. *orat* is Tatian(us)'s *Oratio ad Graecos*; and **Clem**. *str*. is Clement of Alexandria's *Stromateis*; etc.).

Each of these references can be traced in the appropriate volumes of the *Loeb Classical Library*. In addition, a fuller concordance to the writings of Flavius Josephus was produced by K. H. Rengstorf, *A Complete Concordance to Flavius Josephus* (4 vols., 1973-1983).

For those desirous of pursuing their study beyond the era of the Church Fathers, there is E. A. Sophocles' *Greek Lexicon of the Roman and Byzantine Periods* (2 vols.; 1957).

Concordances and lexicons are indispensable reference tools and are available for people at all levels of linguistic attainment. Sooner or later, however, some expertise in Biblical languages becomes a necessity.

A study of material referred to in a concordance precedes the consultation of a lexicon. After tracing the sources mentioned in a concordance and studying the usage of the word in light of the context, a lexicon can be consulted to either validate or correct the work you have done. And because lexicons synthesize material, you may well uncover something passed over by the editors due to the fact that they were dealing with broader issues than the one you have been researching.

A knowledge of the use of concordances and lexicons will prepare you for engaging in one of the most exciting of biblical pursuits, *viz.*, word studies.

How to do a word study will be the focus of our next chapter.

LOOKING AHEAD

1. As you begin to acquire skill in tracing the meaning of words found in the Old Testament, consider the meanings assigned "perish," "way" and "word"[14] in BDB's *A Hebrew and English Lexicon of the Old Testament*, and in Koehler and Baumgarten's *Lexicon in Veteris Testamenti libros* or *Hebrew and Aramaic Lexicon of the Old Testament*. How well has the meaning of each word been analyzed? In what ways does the approach of each of these reference tools differ? Which approach do you prefer? Why?

2. By using Bauer's *Greek-English Lexicon to the New Testament*, trace the different Greek words for "prayer" mentioned in the New Testament. How do they differ from each other? In what contexts have these words been used in the different periods of Greek history? (Where the meaning in classical literature is given in Bauer, check two or three references listed by Bauer in the *Loeb Classical Library*).

3. By using Hatch and Redpath's *Concordance to the Septuagint*, trace the historical references to "Gilgal" and "Shiloh." Probe the significance of these places in the history of God's people and identify the era of each biblical author.

8

Word Studies: Old Testament

With so many linguistic helps available, why should anyone spend time learning how to do Greek and Hebrew word studies?

A little more than a decade ago a Talbot Seminary professor, who was teaching a course in bibliographic research, gave the students an assignment that required each of them to research a particular word in the Old and New Testaments as well as in extra-biblical literature. During the semester he had endeavored to foster an atmosphere of open discussion, and the students felt free to share with him their reactions to the assignment.

One, who was particularly eager to test his new knowledge, could hardly wait for the buzzer to sound so that he could go over to the library and begin work. The response of the other students, however, was more typical of the attitudes of many toward this kind of exercise.

"Why can't we just read up on this word in 'Kittel'"?[15] objected one.

"Because *TDNT* does not discuss this word," was the reply.

"But I'm interested in people," stated another. "They couldn't care less about Greek and Hebrew words and their etymology. The meaning of some obscure word won't make any difference to the way they live."[16]

"True," the professor replied, "but that is where you come in. It's your responsibility to make the Bible come alive, and word studies are one way of doing this."

"But I'm not good at the original languages," responded a third student. "The assignment you have given us intimidates me. What happens if we [really, 'I'] get stuck?"

The question was honestly stated and probably represented the feelings of most of the class. None had ever taken a course in bibliographic research before and, on this account, may have felt overwhelmed.

"I appreciate your candor," was the professor's response:

Perhaps this is a good place at which to assess what we have been doing so far and review those resources which will help you with the assignment.

We began the semester by considering *General Reference Works* covering the whole subject of religion (e.g., M'Clintock and Strong's *Cyclopedia of Biblical, Theological and Ecclesiastical Literature*). The resources we reviewed are encyclopedic in nature and follow a dictionary format in that they are arranged alphabetically by topic. The better encyclopedias contain articles based on the original languages, and you can find philological matters discussed at the beginning of the longer, more scholarly ones.

We then narrowed our focus to Bible dictionaries and encyclopedias (e.g., *Zondervan Pictorial Encyclopedia of the Bible*). Some of these works contain word studies, and some have Hebrew and Greek indices showing where each word has been treated. These provide quick and easy access to those places where the word in question has been discussed.

After this we proceeded on to encyclopedias relating to specific disciplines (e.g., theology [both biblical and systematic], history, philosophy, sociology). A review of your notes will help you find specific references to those works containing philological studies.

Following this, we considered specialized reference tools like Bible atlases, Bible concordances, and Bible commentaries. Sometimes technical Bible commentaries contain helpful data on the nuances of different words. To find out where these words appear in Scripture, you may wish to use a concordance (e.g., Strong's *Exhaustive Concordance of the Bible* or Young's *Analytical Concordance* or the *New American Standard Exhaustive Concordance of the Bible*). You can then check each biblical reference in one or more of the commentaries.

In your study of God's Word it is also important for you to know how to use Hebrew and Greek concordances and lexicons. These we treated during our last class period.

The assignment gives you the opportunity to fall back on and put to practical use some of the resources we have discussed this semester, namely, those technical language tools (i.e., concordances and lexicons) that are essential to a study of the derivation and meaning of words.

Further discussion did not reveal any additional objections, so he proceeded with some specifics.

HEBREW WORD STUDIES

We recognize the limitations of some students who have only a beginner's knowledge of Hebrew (or perhaps none at all), and so this section will deal with the rudiments of:

- *Etymology,* in which we trace historically the origin and development of a word.

- *Usage*, in which we analyze the occurrences of the word in a given body of literature (e.g., the Old Testament) and seek to lay bare the categories of meaning.

- *Verification*, in which we check our findings against reference materials produced by specialists in the field. (Verification is important even when you have used the finest and most scholarly of resources as our illustration of the meaning of *almah* will show.)

In doing a Hebrew word study, it is important to focus on the root form of the word, and then to consider the usage of the word in the Semitic family of languages of which Hebrew is a part. Broadly speaking, the Semitic family "tree" may be divided into East Semitic (Akkadian, with its sub-dialects of Babylonian and Assyrian), South Semitic (Arabic and Ethiopic), and North-Semitic (Canaanite [including Ugaritic], Sinaitic, Phoenecian, etc., and Aramaic with its later offshoot, Syriac). Hebrew belongs to the North-Semitic group.

Etymology

The etymology of a given word not only considers the derivation and history of that word but also its meaning in the cognate Semitic languages. To properly trace the historic development of a given Hebrew term, you should have access to the Gesenius' *Hebrew and English Lexicon of the Old Testament*, edited by F. Brown, S. R. Driver and C. A. Briggs, the *Lexicon in Veteris Testamenti libros*, by L. H. Koehler and W. Baumgarten (and, if possible, its revision), and the *Hebrew and Aramaic Lexicon of the Old Testament*.

Three other works are of the utmost value:

Konkordanz zum hebraischen Alten Testament, by G. Lisowsky

Veteris testamenti concordantiae Habraicae atque Chaldaicae, by S. Mandelkern

Concordance to the Septuagint, by E. Hatch and H. A. Redpath

In a study of the word *dabar* (see BDB, page 180), you will readily see that the editors have gone to considerable lengths to provide the equivalent meaning of a given Hebrew word in related Semitic languages.[17] Building upon what the lexicographers have supplied, you can write down their dictionary definition of the word. This should then be compared with the definition(s) given in Koehler/Baumgartner's *Lexicon*. Differences of meaning should be noted and reflection given as to the possible reasons for these changes. In tracing the possible common origin of a word, the lowest common denominator (or common idea behind the historic development and meaning) of the word should be sought.

Caution needs to be exercised to prevent the inexperienced researcher from too readily adopting opinions based upon inadequate data. In this connection, the warning given as well as the example set by James Barr in *Comparative Philology of the Text of the Old Testament* (1961), is important.

Now, turning to our illustration of *dabar*, we find at the beginning of the discussion there is a listing of the meanings of this word in Arabic (Ar.), Aramaic (Aram.), and Alexandrine manuscript of the Septuagint (A), Assyrian (As.), and Syriac (Syr.), et cetera. Because Ras Shamra (ancient Ugarit) has been discovered in more recent times, the important contribution of Ugaritic studies to Old Testament literature will not be found in BDB and will have to be obtained from other sources (e.g., Cyrus Gordon's *Ugaritic Textbook*).

With some idea of the meaning of the word under consideration, it will be of value to you if you will now take note of the derived terms which may illustrate the basic idea, the occasions when the word is used, the people involved, the synonyms, antonyms or homonyms employed in different forms of Hebrew parallelism, and the situations giving rise to its usage. Then, having examined as thoroughly as possible the dictionary definition of the word and its meaning in cognate Semitic languages, it is appropriate to consider in depth and detail its *usage* in the canonical Scriptures of the Old Testament.

Usage

The *usage* of a term is of the utmost importance in determining its meaning. To survey its usage, you will need to use one or more concordances. Students lacking a knowledge of Hebrew that permits them to use the more technical reference works will find Strong's *Exhaustive Concordance of the Bible* or the *New American Standard Exhaustive Concordance of the Bible* helpful, particularly if the number listed against each entry is checked with the brief definition of the word in the index at the back. Likewise, many have found Young's *Analytical Concordance to the Bible* to be of inestimable value. However, because a study of a word must be undertaken in accordance with its root, it may be necessary to resort to the *Englishman's Hebrew and Chaldee Concordance of the Old Testament*. All of these works (with the exception of the *New American Standard Exhaustive Concordance of the Bible*) are based on the text of the Authorized (or King James) Version.

Indispensable tools for the student with a knowledge of Hebrew include:

Lisowsky's *Konkordanz zum hebraischen Alten Testament,* with the meaning of each word given in Latin, German and English. The value of this work lies in its listing of every Scripture verse in which a particular Hebrew word is found.

Mandelkern's *Veteris testamenti concordantiae Habraicae atque*

Chaldaicae, which lists each distinct form separately and provides the researcher with references for each root of a word; and for the Greek of the LXX.

Hatch and Redpath's *Concordance to the Septuagint*, a work that makes available parallel references to the Greek text of the LXX.

The procedure to be followed is to look up each occurrence of the word, evaluate its usage

in light of the context, and decide upon its precise meaning. When this has been done, the different usages may be grouped together into semantic categories for further study.

For example, the verb *bahan* is found to mean "to examine, to try, to prove." Its derivatives include "testing," "watchtower," "siege towers" and "assayer."

The occurrence of *bahan* is chiefly in the books of Job, Psalms and Jeremiah (though its usage is not confined to these writings). In addition, it occurs in parallelism with *nasa* ("to put to the test, to tempt") and *sarap* ("to smelt, to refine"). What then is its basic meaning? *Bahan* would seem to denote examination with a view to determining the essential qualities or integrity of a person, a group of people, a place or a thing. On closer examination, the usage of *bahan* generally has God as the Subject, whereas *nasa* almost always has man as the subject; and *sarap* is used exclusively in a religious sense with God as the Subject and man as the object. Three of the references to *bahan* reverse the general order and have God as the One being tested (e.g., Psalm 95:9; Malachi 3:10, 15) by the attitude or conduct of His people.

A further observation of the usage of *bahan* (which may be made on the basis of an investigation of the text) is that *nasa* and *sarap* seem to denote the attainment of knowledge through testing, whereas *bahan* seems to point to the acquisition of knowledge through learning or intuition.

Similar studies may be done of key Hebrew words like *hesed*, "lovingkindness"; *qadosh* "holy"; *tselem* "image"; *tsedeq*, "righteousness"; *gibbor*, "[man or woman] of valor, mighty [warrior]", and many, many more. Each word will be found to possess a fascination all its own, and the insights derived from such a study will readily lend themselves to homiletic sub-division, sermonic illustration, and practical application.

Of further interest is the comparison of the Hebrew text with the Old Testament in Greek (LXX). For this you will need Hatch and Redpath's *Concordance to the Septuagint.* In this connection it is interesting to compare the Greek translation of Isaiah 7:14 with the Hebrew original. Attention, of course, is focused on the word *almah*, "young woman," and we are told by some lexicographers that if Isaiah had intended us to understand "virgin" he would have used the term *bethulah*. With this judgment most lexicons agree. But are they correct?

The real questions are: How did Ahaz, and the ancient Hebrews from the time of Isaiah, and the Jews of Jesus' day, understand Isaiah's prophecy? And how did the Jews who translated their own Scriptures into Greek understand the usage of *almah* in this passage?

Interestingly enough, the Greek text of Rahlfs' *Septuaginta: id est, Vetus Testamentum graece iuxta LXX interpretes* (2 vols.; 3d ed.; 1965) uses the word *parthenos* as the Hellenistic equivalent of *almah*, and *parthenos* unequivocally means "virgin." Further corroboration of this comes from another Jew named Levi (or Matthew). He was a learned man and a former employee of Rome. When quoting Isaiah's prophecy he unashamedly used *parthenos* to describe Christ's miraculous conception by Mary (Matthew 1:23).

Reference to the Septuagint provides many such sidelights on the terms employed by the writers of Scripture. Its use, therefore, should not be neglected!

Verification

Because the most valuable lexicons may, on occasion, be misleading (as in the case of *almah* cited above), you will need to verify your findings. In doing so, reference may be made to a variety of source materials alluded to in earlier chapters. These include commentaries like the *NICOT* and the *NICNT*, and exegetical works like the *International Critical Commentary*. The *ICC*, while not conservative, may prove helpful to the researcher in either broadening his/her perspective on the usage of a word or providing insights into the way the meanings of a word may by analyzed. Other suggestions may be obtained from *The Minister's Library*.

By regularly evaluating the material contained in lexicons as well as *TDOT* and *TWOT*, you will be able to verify the results of your own research. The product of your investigation will enrich your own life and ministry. This will be evidenced by the assurance you bring to your exposition of the text, the interest that you are able to generate in the study of the Old Testament, and the way in which seemingly irrelevant issues suddenly take on contemporary significance.

LOOKING AHEAD

By utilizing English and Greek concordances, study the usage of words like *stephanos*, "wreath, crown," and *sundoulos*, "fellow-slave," in the New Testament as well as the Septuagint. Seek to ascertain the basic meaning of each word as well as its spiritual significance.

9

Word Studies: New Testament

A preacher cannot minister effectively without having an in-depth understanding of the meaning of words and terms used in the Bible. John 3:16, for example, requires at the very least a working definition of *agape* love, and the Beatitudes which begin the "Sermon on the Mount" (Matthew 5:1-12) necessitate a understanding of the meaning of "discipleship," "blessed," "poor in spirit," "kingdom of heaven," "mourn," "comfort," "gentle (or humble or meek)," "righteousness," et cetera, if they are to be properly interpreted and properly understood. The great teachings of the Christian faith--justification, forgiveness, redemption, reconciliation, propitiation, sanctification, glorification--require of each believer an understanding of their meaning.

A study of specific words used in the New Testament may be expected to do the following for us:

Aid in providing an enriched perspective and an in-depth understanding of the theological and practical importance of the word in question.

Serve as a check on the lexical aids that we all must use.

Reveal to us the many-faceted riches of God's Word.

Word studies do *not* take the place of exegesis (involving the comparison of different documents, grammar, syntax, the theological background of each writer, the occasion of the book, its purpose, the context of the passage, and the characteristics of the writer), but they are basic and fundamental to an accurate interpretation of the text. The procedure for doing a study of a New Testament word is essentially the same as for the Old Testament, only the resource tools are different.

For example, a word study should be based upon the *historical* development of the usage of the word. As mentioned in an earlier chapter this involves an awareness of the phases in the development of the Greek language. Two distinct phases are of particular interest to us: classical and Koine (or common Greek, with the latter embracing the translating of the Old Testament into Greek, the writing of the New Testament, and the sermons and books written during the Apostolic age).

In addition, a word study should be *inductive*. It is the inquirer's responsibility to determine all possible meanings of the word being studied, and then to categorize their meaning in accordance with the time period and the situation that gave rise to its use.

GREEK WORD STUDIES

Etymology

In undertaking a study of a New Testament word, the first prerequisite is that it be in accordance with its root form. Only then can it be studied historically. The study of root forms is complex and difficult. It is also complicated by the inclusion of prefixes, suffixes, and infixes. And there is always the danger that inexperienced researchers will take the root form of a word and its meaning as the only meaning. The meaning of the root is not necessarily the same as its derived forms. The true meaning of a word can only be found in its usage. Of great help is *A Greek Grammar of the New Testament* by F. Blass and A. Debrunner, and the *Grammar of New Testament Greek* (especially Vol. 2, pp. 267-410) by J. H. Moulton and W. F. Howard.

Once the root form of a word has been ascertained (perhaps through the use of an excellent work such as *The New Linguistic and Exegetical Key to the Greek New Testament* by C. L. Rogers, Jr., and his son, C. L. Rogers III), the process of tracing the usage of a word through the historical stages of its development can begin. The meaning can then be ascertained by using:

Liddell and Scott's *Greek-English Lexicon* for the classical period. By checking references to specific words in the *Loeb Classical Library* or some other translation that includes book, chapter and line (somewhat similar to a play) to facilitate the location of the word in question.

Hatch and Redpath's *Concordance to the Septuagint of the Old Testament in Greek.*

Moulton and Geden's *Concordance to the Greek Testament* or the *Computer concordance to the Novum Testamentum Graece/Computer-Konkordanz zum Novum Testamentum Graece* for word usage in the New Testament.

Moulton and Milligan's *Vocabulary of the Greek Testament* for the usage of Koine words found in the papyri; and

Lampe's *Patristic Greek Lexicon* for illustrations of the meaning attached to words after the period of the Apostles.

But why is it necessary to trace the meaning of a word through the different stages of history?

Over time words change in meaning. A historical approach, therefore, will alert us to these changes. For example, in the New Testament, *eritheia* is the word for "strife" or "selfish ambition." This, however, was not always its meaning. In the process of time its original meaning degenerated so that in each of its seven occurrences in the New Testament it is used of contention or the abuse of ambition which undermines the cause of Christ and impedes the work of the Church.

Eritheia originally came from the root *eris* meaning "day laborer" (specifically one associated with the wool industry), and meant "labor," or more pointedly, "labor for wages." It involved doing a day's work well in order to receive a day's pay.

How then did *eritheia* come to mean "contention, strife, or selfish ambition"?

The point of departure from the healthy to an unhealthy connotation of the word seems to be in the motive of the laborers. There arose a series of circumstances in which the emphasis was no longer placed on *honest* labor. Instead, the attitude of the workers seemed to be, "What can I get out of this situation?" Less and less quality work was done, and more and more was demanded. This, of course, led to squabbles and power struggles between an employer and a united band of employees. (All of this bears a striking resemblance to labor/management disputes today, doesn't it?) It is not surprising, therefore, that eventually the word came to be applied to one who would exploit a situation (by causing strife) for his own advantage.

Quite obviously, a historical approach to the meaning of a term lends a unique fascination to our study of the New Testament. It can also make the application of truth to life most interesting!

Context

Second, the word we choose to investigate must be studied inductively in its varying contexts before its nuances or meaning during a particular period of time, or use by a specific author, can be ascertained. In other words, *induction* must precede *deduction*.

In an earlier chapter we also made reference to T. J. Conant's famous work *The Meaning and Use of Baptizein* (1860/1977) in which he examined each occurrence of the word "to baptize" in classical and Hellenistic

Greek to determine its true meaning. This was most appropriate for a term that has caused such division in the church. Quite apart from its meaning when considered as an ordinance of the church, Thomas Conant found that in literature outside the New Testament *baptizein* was used of ritual washing, a ship which sank, a person whose head was held under water until he drowned, and union with a person quite apart from any sacramental association.

What then did he find to be the common denominator of all these meanings?

An inductive study of the word *baptizein* led to the conclusion that its basic meaning is "identification" (sometimes with disastrous results). When applied to the New Testament, this "working definition" of the word was found to be consistent. The ancient Israelites were identified with Moses in the events of the Exodus (1 Corinthians 10:2); proselytes to Judaism immersed themselves, signifying their identification with the people of Israel; the Jews at the time of John the Baptist identified themselves with the message he proclaimed; the Lord Jesus, by baptism, identified Himself with those whom He came to save; and the people who believed the message of the coming of the Kingdom which Christ preached as being "at hand," were baptized to demonstrate their identification with it.

Once the *meaning* of baptism has been established, we are then free to consider the *mode* by which it is/was to be applied as well as the *subjects* to whom the rite was administered. In the case of "baptism" the *mode* should not be confused with its basic *meaning*!

Verification

Due to the fact that even the finest of lexicons may be misleading, it is wise to verify the results of your inductive research by consulting several sources (e.g., Kittel's *TDNT* and Brown's *NIDNTT*), as well as the ablest of commentaries (that can easily be traced via *The Minister's Library*. By evaluating the critical data contained in these reference works, or the comments by the author of a technical commentary, you will be able to verify your own research. Only by following the process described above will you, as a part of a new generation of Bible students, be able to modify and advance the work of those who have preceded you.

LOOKING AHEAD

Having concluded our study of *general reference works*, we are now in a position to consider two related topics: (1) The further collection of data from books, periodicals and unpublished materials; and (2) the process by which topics can be refined.

In preparation for the next chapter, research the standard systematic theologies and consider all the sub-divisions of Christology. How would you go about researching the two natures of Christ? Make a list of the resources you would consult. Add to your list works cited in the footnotes of the treatises on theology that you have consulted. As far as possible, try and identify the theological perspective of each writer (e.g., his/her theological position [liberal, conservative, Calvinistic, Arminian]), and then his/her denominational background, level of scholarship, together with evident strengths and any apparent weaknesses.

10

Online Searching

In the preceding chapters we covered *general reference works*--those research tools that will enable you to explore the parameters of virtually any biblical or theological topic. And we've included other disciplines of related interest (e.g., philosophy, education, counseling). From these resources you should be able to ascertain who has made a contribution to the advancement of knowledge in a particular area, and when and where this was done; and you should also be able to evaluate any biases which may be present. In addition, you have also learned how to do Hebrew and Greek word studies. Without such a foundation the value of your work may be reduced considerably and accuracy may be lost.

Now, having gained some familiarity with general reference works, you are in a position to "graduate" to the next level where you will be able to explore online resources that will help you find out what has been written on the topic you are researching. In doing so, you will be moving from the *general* to the *specific*. In subsequent chapters we will concentrate on unpublished materials like theses and dissertations.

REFINING YOUR TOPIC

There is an important step, however, that comes between general and specific resources—one that is often overlooked. It involves refining your terminology and, perhaps, narrowing the focus of your topic.

Because books in libraries are cataloged according to their content, it is important for you to know something about the subject categories that have been assigned to them. The primary resource available to librarians in the United States (i.e., catalogers who are responsible for assigning *approved* subject headings to each book) is the multi-volume *Library of Congress Subject Headings*. This very necessary resource tool is in the process of continuous revision.

The subject headings relating to the content of a given book are either typed on a card or, more than likely, entered into a computer. The data are then made available in a format that will enable students to quickly and easily ascertain the library's holdings on a particular subject. Whatever the format—cards or a computer catalog—the data are collected under three primary headings: (1) author or main entry; (2) title; (3) subject heading(s); and, where necessary, joint authors and/or editors. We are primarily interested in the subject headings and how those who catalog and classify the library's holdings are able to use them.

Now, take for example the subject of Christology. The student who was asked to research the two natures of Christ and checked the catalog under "CHRISTOLOGY" (see chapter 1), was tempted to conclude that the library did not have holdings in this area. Had he checked the *Library of Congress Subject Headings* he would have found an entry in light type under "Christology" advising him to check under "**Jesus Christ**."

Jesus Christ is in boldface type, meaning that this is an approved subject heading. Under **Jesus Christ** he would have found general Library of Congress classification numbers (*BT198—590*), and this would have directed him to the area of the library where these books are located. Subdivisions under **Jesus Christ** in the *Library of Congress Subject Headings* occupy the next four pages. By browsing through these sub-divisions the student could have refined his topic while at the same time sharpening the focus of his terminology.

In addition, under most headings there are symbols. In place of the previous "See" references, researchers now have a series of different letters: NT, BF, UF, USE, RT, and SA.

NT stands for "Narrower Term" and intimates that the subject matter may be found under more restricted nomenclature. BT is the exact opposite. It advises the researcher that material is to be found under a "Broader Term." The two terms USE and UF are primarily for librarians. USE references are made from an unauthorized or non-preferred term to an authorized or preferred one. UF is an abbreviation for "Used for" and proceeds a term no longer used as an approved subject heading. Finally, RT directs users to a "Related Term" which may prove more helpful in research than the one in vogue in books written by specialists in a particular discipline or used by a teacher (e.g., "Christology" is a commonly used term, but **Jesus Christ** [followed by a dash and a descriptive term] is where you will most likely find the information you seek). And SA, "See Also," is designed to guide researchers to source materials that will add depth to their field of investigation.

In order to master the *Library of Congress Subject Headings* it will pay you to spend time browsing through one or more of these volumes in your school's library. You will find your librarian quite willing to explain the value of these books to you. And by using approved subject headings you will be able to find books in your library that otherwise might elude your investigation.

Let us take a closer look at the heading **Jesus Christ**. Under "**Jesus Christ**—Natures" there is a "SA" (See Also) reference directing you to additional areas: "**Hypostatic Union**" and "**Jesus Christ**--Person and offices**." You now have three areas to investigate: **Jesus Christ**--Natures; **Hypostatic Union** (including Hypostatic Union--History of doctrines); and **Jesus Christ**--Person and offices.

Under **Hypostatic Union** a single classification number is given (*BT 205*). This is more specific than the ones assigned the broad area of Christology (*viz., BT 198-590*).

ONLINE SEARCHING

With a clearer idea of the approved library terminology relating to a given topic, you are now in a position to proceed to the next stage of your investigation, namely, accessing information via online resources.

The proliferation of electronic publishing, the digitizing of libraries of printed materials, and the rapid growth of the Internet, render this chapter out-of-date before it is written. Yet its general subject matter is important no matter what innovations become popular next week or next month or next year. And you, as a theological researcher, face the same staggering information overload as everyone else. Keeping up with technological change seems impossible, but we must learn to make the best use of the tools of technology and to "enjoy the ride."

In this section of the chapter we will give a brief overview of online resources that may be useful for theological research. Some of these, however, either have been or will be discussed in greater detail in other chapters. We will also cover basic "searching strategies" of finding relevant information. Here's our outline:

- How to find books and dissertations
- How to find articles
- How to find theological resources through the Internet
- World Wide Web resources
- Mailing Lists
- Bible software

How to Find Books and Dissertations

The first place one looks for books in today's library is the Library Catalog or OPAC (Online Public Access Catalog). OPACs have replaced card catalogs in most libraries. The library catalog tells you what books, dissertations and other materials can be found in the library, along with their location and availability. Bibliographic records give you the author, title, date of publication, and other information such as Library of Congress Subject Headings.

As was pointed out earlier in this chapter, Library of Congress Subject Headings are assigned each book. If you search the catalog by subject heading, you can find all of the books that were assigned that subject heading. All you have to do is determine which subject heading(s) pertain to your topic.

Online catalogs for most libraries can be accessed through the Internet, either via Telnet or the World Wide Web (WWW). In addition, some useful sites for finding catalogs are: Hytelnet [www.lights.com/hytelnet], Libweb [sunsite.Berkeley.EDU/Libweb], and WebCATS [www.lights.com/webcats].

The best ways to conduct comprehensive searches for books or dissertations are by searching the *WorldCat* database in *FirstSearch*, available through the OCLC (Online Computer Library Center), or by searching the *RLIN Bibliographic Database*. *WorldCat* allows searching of more than 31,000 libraries simultaneously, and *RLIN* combines the catalogs of over 250 university libraries. Before you begin searching, take time to read the "Help" screens. Spending five minutes reading the "Help" screens can save five hours of searching time.

Some techniques that we have found helpful in getting relevant results in searching *WorldCat* are: browsing indexes, setting limits, combining search fields, and searching by subject heading.

Examples:

Browsing Indexes: **lewis c s** (Author)—avoids records from other authors named Lewis.

Setting Limits: **1990-** (Year)**, books** (Document type) and **English** (Language)—limits the search to books published in English from 1990 to the present.

Combining search fields: **grudem** (Author) and **systematic theology** (Title)—yields the precise record.

Subject Heading: **Bible Inspiration** (Subject) gives books on the inspiration of Scripture.

Selected book chapters and dissertations can also be found by searching the *ATLA Religion Database*, which is published by the American Theological Library Association. Dissertations can be found in the *Dis-*

sertation Abstracts International database. Recently published books can be discovered by searching *Books in Print*.

There are several Internet sites that are good for finding books. Some of the best are: Amazon.com [www.amazon.com], barnesandnoble.com [www.bn.com], Powell's Books [www.powells.com], and Dove Booksellers [www.dovebook.com].

How to Find Journal Articles

How easy is it to find articles in the broad area of religion? The most logical places to conduct online searching for articles are the *ATLA Religion Database* and *Religious & Theological Abstracts*. Other useful online CD-ROM databases include: *Old Testament Abstracts, New Testament Abstracts, Catholic Periodical and Literature Index (CPLI)*, and *Zeitschrifteninhaltsdienst Theologie*. Useful Internet databases include: *ProQuest Research Library, Academic Search Elite* (EBSCOhost), *Expanded Academic ASAP* (InfoTrac SearchBank), and *LEXIS-NEXIS Academic Universe*.

The *ProQuest Religion* database offers access to full text articles in religion, theology, and biblical studies. And ATLA will expand its database by adding full text journals through its ATLAS: ATLA Serials project.

Our extensive use of the *ATLA Religion Database* on CD-ROM (DOS version) has led us to the frequent use of the following search strategies and techniques that may also be helpful for searching the Internet versions:

- Browse the indexes for any of the searchable fields. Browsing the index for the Subject Heading (Descriptor) field gives the searcher a list of terms, that increases precision in finding relevant articles. The online thesaurus of the printed *Religion Indexes: Thesaurus* allows the searcher to find and use the correct subject headings. For instance, we have found students using the search term "pastors" and finding very little of value because the database uses "clergy" as a subject heading covering pastors. The thesaurus also reveals that the term "Indians of North America" is used instead of "Native Americans." And a good way to find articles on the book of Romans is to use the subject heading "Bible (NT) Romans." In general, it is best to search the Subject Heading field before searching by keyword to reduce the number of irrelevant records.

- Boolean search operators (e.g., the use of AND, OR, NOT) are especially helpful in the Keyword and Subject Heading fields. Some examples are: "women AND leadership", "ministry OR church work", and "Indians NOT American."

- Combined field searching is automatically set up by default as Boolean AND searching. This is what a typical combined field search may look like:

  Subject heading: spiritual formation
  Language: English
  Record type: Article
  Year: 1990...1999

- Truncation or wild card can reduce the need for multiple searches or the use of the Boolean OR. Use "child*" to search for child, child's, children, and childhood. Use "Gen 3:*" in the Scripture Reference field for all records on Genesis 3 instead of using Gen. 3:1, Gen. 3:2, et cetera.

- Don't forget the Person as Subject field. Researchers looking for articles on the "body of Christ" in the Subject Heading field may be frustrated. The desired subject "Jesus Christ—Mystical Body" is to be found under Person as Subject.

- We suggest using the Full Display when viewing records (in the CD-ROM version). The Full Display gives complete titles, helpful subject headings for additional searches, and notes. The Standard and Extended lists are most helpful when searching for a known item.

The main advantage of searching for articles in the *Religious & Theological Abstracts* CD-ROM is the abstracts that are a part of each record. Search words are highlighted—enabling easy evaluation of articles. *RTA* allows Boolean searching of five searchable fields. The easiest way to search is by using keywords in the "Full Text" field, and combining them with AND, OR, NEAR, and NOT. You can also use these Boolean terms for combining the search fields (Title, Author, Year, or Bible Citation). *ATLA* is the larger of the two databases, and it gives the searcher more options for finding relevant records (please see our discussion of *ATLA* in Chapter 11).

How to Find Theological Resources Throught The Internet

Of what value is the Internet when it comes to research in religion? Despite much of the futuristic hype about the Internet replacing the library, most theological resources can be found only in print or microform--*in a library*. Digitization of library collections, however, will increasingly provide electronic access to more and more materials. Today you can search the catalogs of most libraries through the Internet. Eventually you should be able to search the entire collections—every page of every book—of most libraries from your personal computer. (But don't hold your breath waiting. Only a small percentage of the 18 million books in the Library of Congress has been digitized.) The full texts of thousands of electronic journals and digitized books are already available in most theological libraries. We expect that within a few years the majority of journals indexed by *ATLA* and *RTA* will be accessible in full text. The technology is available, but concerns such as copyright and cost may prolong the process.

The Internet provides access to a rapidly growing number of resources useful for theological research. Examples of these resources are: books, journals, and newsletters; ancient texts; bibliographies; computer software; home pages for Christian ministries, churches, and mission organizations; Christian book stores and antiquarian dealers; e-mail lists and bulletin boards; college and seminary home pages; publishers' catalogs; and library catalogs.

But someone will ask, "How can we use the Internet to find theological resources?" We will briefly cover some search tools and search strategies for conducting theological research through the Internet.

Subject Directories. Subject directories, subject catalogs, or indexes enable searching the World Wide Web by topic or subject. The most popular and useful subject directory is Yahoo [www.yahoo.com]. Yahoo uses "Surfing Yahoos" to review and to categorize web sites by topic and subject. You can pick and click on a hierarchical arrangement of subjects, or you can conduct a keyword search of the Yahoo website. For example, to find theological resources via the subject hierarchy, click on Society and Culture: Religion, and browse the list of subjects. This is not a very efficient search method, however, and so we recommend typing search terms in the search window. Before conducting a site search of Yahoo, take a few minutes to read the Help on Search and Advanced Search Syntax pages.

Search Engines. Search engines enable keyword searching of the Internet. Each search engine searches and stores Internet pages in different ways, so you will never get the same results from any two search engines. The most common error we observe is the searcher who conducts a simple keyword search which retrieves tens of thousands of websites, and is satisfied with the first ten regardless of their value. We recommend that researchers become very familiar with at least two search engines. This means reading the "Help" or "Advanced Search" instructions for these engines, and taking the time to practice searching for and finding relevant results. Remember: *Each search engine or search tool is unique!*

As we write this book our favorite search engines are AltaVista [www.altavista.com], HotBot [www.hotbot.com], and Northern Light [www.northernlight.com]. But by the time you read our suggestions, new and better search engines may have been developed. For the sake of illustration we shall use <u>Alta Vista</u> as an example. First, we recommend the use of the "Advanced Search," which allows the use of search statements that are more likely to achieve relevant results. The following strategies can be used for <u>AltaVista</u> or any search engine:

- *Boolean and proximity operators.* Use "AND, +, OR, NOT,-" or "NEAR, WITH, ADJ" (if available). Here are a few examples: **Creation AND Evolution** (both words must be present), **Theology OR Doctrine** (either word must be present. **Scriptures NOT Apocrypha** (Apocrypha cannot be present). **Creation NEAR Evolution** (both words must be within a certain number of words of each other). **Covenant WITH Theology** (both words must be within a certain number of words of each other, and they must be in this order).

- *Phrase searching.* "**Biblical Studies**" or "**Commentaries for Biblical Expositors.**" Quotation marks or other punctuation marks are used to indicate that the words must appear next to each other, in this order.

- *Truncation.* **Theol*** could be used to include theology, theological, theologians, et cetera. Truncation allows for searching plurals and various suffixes.

- *Field searching.* We have found that searching by title can greatly reduce large numbers of irrelevant entries, and produce relevant results. **Title: "Biblical Studies"** assures that the term "Biblical Studies" will appear in the title, and it is most likely that that will be the subject of the sites retrieved. Title searching can also cause you to miss your desired site. For example, if you are looking for the story of the starfish and the little boy, these words may not appear in the title. **Url:edu** will limit your search to educational sites in the USA, but remember that this will also exclude educational sites in Canada and other countries.

- *Nesting.* **Theology AND (Covenant or Dispensational)** will yield results for both kinds of theology.

- *Synonyms.* Use the least common words as search terms. Use nesting to add synonyms and to increase the number of hits.

- *New search.* If you get too many hits or irrelevant records, modify your search strategy and try a new search. Conduct numerous searches until you are able to get relevant results.

- *Evaluate.* Evaluate the authority of the sources and their accuracy.

Don't assume that everything on the Internet is true. Several websites are helpful in evaluating Internet research results.

Thinking Critically About World Wide Web Resources, by Esther Grassian of the UCLA College Library.
[www.library.ucla.edu/libraries/college/instruct/web/critical.html]

Evaluating Information Found on the Internet from Johns Hopkins University Library.
[www.milton.mse.jhu.edu.8001/research/education/net.html]

Evaluating Web Resources, by Jane Alexander and Marsha Tate of Widener University.
[www2.widener.edu/Wolfgram-Memorial Library/webeval.htm]

Meta-Search Engines. Meta-search engines search the Internet using several search engines (and subject directories) simultaneously. They allow only simple search strategies and produce limited results. Our favorite meta-search engine is MetaCrawler [www.go2net.com/search.html].

World Wide Web Resources

A plethora of websites with potential usefulness to theological researchers can be found through the Internet. For the sake of giving some starting points for Internet research, we offer the following list of sites that we have found to be helpful:

Religious Studies Web Guide. "This web site focuses on resources of use to researchers involved in the academic study of religion." Compiled by Saundra Lipton and Cheryl Adams. [www.acs.ucalgary.ca/~lipton]

The Wabash Center Guide to Internet Resources for Teaching and Learning in Theology and Religion. "A selective, annotated guide to a variety of electronic resources of interest to those who are teaching or studying religion and theology at the graduate or undergraduate level." [www.wabashcenter.wabash.edu/Internet/front.htm]

Finding God in Cyberspace: A Guide to Religious Studies Resources on the Internet. "This guide provides a selective listing of Internet resources of interest to religious studies scholars and students of religion." [www.fontbonne.edu/libserv/fgic/contents.htm]

Not Just Bibles: A Guide to Christian Resources on the Internet. Highly recommended—one of the most comprehensive guides to evangelical Christian resources available through the Internet. [www.iclnet.org/pub/resources/christian-resources.html]

Guide to Early Church Documents. A list of sites "relating to the early church, including canonical creeds, the writings of the Apostolic Fathers, and other historical texts relevant to church history." [www.iclnet.org/pub/resources/christian-history.html]

A Guide to Christian Literature on the Internet. Compilation of "Internet accessible literature related to Classical Christianity (a term coined by C. S. Lewis to describe a theology which affirms the importance of a transforming faith in Christ as God and Savior)." [www.iclnet.org/pub/resources/christian-books.html]

Theology Website. Collection of Christian theological information and resources compiled by the historical theology department at Trinity Evangelical Divinity School and Trinity International University. [www.theologywebsite.com]

Computer-Assisted Theology: Internet Resources for the Study and Teaching of Theology. Extensive annotated listing of theological resources, compiled and annotated by Michael Fraser. [info.ox.ac.uk/ctitext/theology]

Index to Interpreting Ancient Manuscripts. "Study of the ancient manuscripts upon which the New Testament is based." (www.stg.brown.edu/prohects/mss/index.html]

Center for the Advancement of Paleo Orthodoxy. Resource for Reformed theology and evangelical scholarship. [capo.org]

Resource Pages for Biblical Studies. A guide to a variety of resources for biblical studies. [www.hivolda.no/asf/kkf/rel-stud.html]

Christian Classical Ethereal Library. Classical Christian books in electronic format (public domain) compiled by Harry Plantinga at Wheaton College. [ccel.wheaton.edu]

Internet Resources for the Study of Judaism and Christianity. Useful site for finding links to Jewish and Christian resources. Includes "Course Materials" from religious studies courses. Compiled by Jay Treat at the University of Pennsylvania. [ccat.sas.upenn.edu/rs/resources.html]

The Ecole Initiative. "A hypertext encyclopedia of early church history." [cedar.evansville.edu/~ecoleweb]

Biblical Studies Foundation. "The Biblical Studies Foundation is a non-profit organization founded for the purpose of distributing sound, evangelical Bible study materials in electronic format." [www.bible.org]

Theological Research Exchange Network (TREN). "TREN is a library of over 7,800 theological theses/dissertation titles representing research from as many as 70 different institutions. TREN also makes available conference papers presented at annual meetings of several academic societies." [www.tren.com]

Goshen: Global Online Service Helping Evangelize Nations. A searchable directory of Christian resources, ministries, and organizations. [www.goshen.net/WebDirectory]

Seminary and school of theology home pages are also good places to conduct theological research. We have found Yale Divinity School Library to be a most useful website, and especially the Yale University Library Research Guide for Christianity [www.library.yale.edu/div/xtiangde.htm]. Theological researchers can also benefit from the home page for the American Theological Library Association [www.atla.com], where the monthly Atlantis Reference Reviews provide critiques of recently published books.

Mailing Lists

Mailing lists, electronic conferences, E-mail discussion lists, or listservs are a useful application of e-mail. Mailing lists allow a group of people with a common interest to communicate with each other and to ask questions or to share information. Numerous mailing lists exist which may be useful for theological research.

Two convenient WWW sites for finding mailing lists in theology are Dr. Michael Fraser's Shortlist of Email Forums for Theologians and the section on "Mail Based Services" at Not Just Bibles. To subscribe, simply send an email message to the mailing list address, leave the subject blank, and type SUBSCRIBE plus the name of the list, plus your name in the message area. Please read the directions carefully before you subscribe, and keep a copy of the acceptance message for future use.

An example of how to subscribe to the e-mail list for the American Theological Library Association:

E-mail address: lyris@lyris.hds.harvard.edu

Subject: (leave blank)

Message: SUBSCRIBE ATLANTIS (followed by your name).

Bible Software

Bible software CD-ROMs are proving themselves to be increasingly useful tools for theological research. There are numerous choices from many software publishers, who have filled their CD-ROMs with searchable electronic books. These are virtual library reference collections. High end software packages may include many useful works such as:

Biblica Hebraica Stuttgartensia (Hebrew Old Testament) with Westminster Morphology

Nestle-Aland 27th/United Bible Societies 4th edition Greek New Testament with GRAMCORD Morphology

Septuagint (LXX), (Alfred Rahlfs' edition) with CCAT Morphology

Textus Receptus (Scrivener's 1881 and Stephen's 1550) Greek texts

Strong's Concordance with Enhanced Lexicon

A Greek-English Lexicon of the New Testament and Other Early Christian Literature (Bauer, Arndt, Gingrich, and Danker)

Tense, Voice, Mood (Greek and Hebrew)

Complete Works of Josephus

Early Church Fathers

Several versions of the Bible

Commentaries, Lexicons, Concordances, Bible Dictionaries, Theological works, Handbooks, Atlases, etc

Each Bible Software package has a unique user interface and search program. High end programs can search all books, or books you select, at the same time. And you can search in Greek, Hebrew, or English, using Boolean operators or truncation. Just a few of the many helpful features are: the tiling of Greek or Hebrew texts next to the KJV or NASB; concordance and lexicon searches; displays of tense, voice, and mood; and cutting and pasting to the clipboard.

Most Bible Software companies have adopted the STEP (Standard Template for Electronic Publishing), which allows the user to read STEP-compatible books published by other companies. The *Logos Library System* is not STEP-compatible, but it offers the user a powerful search engine and a rapidly growing number of books, which can all be searched simultaneously.

Some considerations when purchasing Bible software are: cost, technical support, availability of book titles, searchability features, warranties, and upgrading. Several publishers have Web sites where you can find out more about the product, or download a demo. Some of the popular Bible Software packages have electronic conferences or listservs where you can contact other users of the same product. *Christian Computing Magazine* and *Christianity Online* frequently provide informative reviews of Bible Software.

REVIEW

In this chapter we have covered a variety of themes of importance to you as a researcher:

We began with the possible need to narrow down a topic. At the same time, you learned about using approved terminology if you are to obtain the best results from your consultation of your library's catalog; and

We then surveyed a variety of online databases that provide easy access to information of importance to you in your studies.

The ease with which you can now begin to gather data and do your research—not to mention the time you will save—should begin to pay dividends in qualitatively better reports and greater depth in your research assignments.

11

Specific Resource Tools: Indexes and Abstracts Part 1

Frederick Jackson Turner, in his insightful book *The Frontier in American History,* described the values which he believed have been characteristic of past generations of Americans. These included a deeply ingrained sense of personal freedom, strong determination, rugged individualism, an inquisitive nature, and the ability to develop creative solutions to perplexing problems. It was Turner's belief that these values were in large measure lost when the frontier closed, and that this signaled an end to "the American Way of Life."

We do not believe that the values that have characterized Americans in years past have been entirely lost. Change in the way we live has not eliminated the desire for personal freedom, or the sense of determination which impels men and women forward, or the rugged individualism that energizes some people to strive to rise above their environment, or the desire to pursue new areas of knowledge and in this way creatively apply what has been learned to the solution of current problems. If these had been lost, how could we have placed men on the moon or sent satellites into outer space? To be sure the process of socialization has tended to breed conformity, but these same pressures were present in the days of the early frontier (only in different ways). History records only the exploits of the bold and the daring, and seldom acknowledges the work done by the plodders and the persevering. The "maverick" quality is still present in the American way of life. Now, however, it is evident in less dramatic ways.

One of the areas of American life that demands the criteria so aptly described by Turner is research. And all the values mentioned by him must be inherent in the researcher if he or she is to be successful.

During the 1960s and 70s when we pursued our seminary studies, we knew what it was like to spend hours upon hours in the library taking journals off the shelf and consulting the index of each one to see if it contained any information that was relevant to our research. Indexes and abstracts were only just beginning to be published. Few libraries subscribed to *Biblica*, largely because few librarians knew of its existence. The *Index to Religious Periodical Literature* (*IRPL*) indexed less than one hundred journals. It, and *Religious and Theological Abstracts* (*RTA*), had begun the task of classifying journal articles by subject so recently, neither of them could boast of a large reservoir of information. Now, however, the entire picture has changed. Numerous indexes are being published, and subjects are being covered more comprehensively. Most of the popular indexes and abstracts are published in the electronic format, which allows searching of all citations, in all volumes, in all years, simultaneously.

The value of these new databases of information is illustrated in the experience of a friend of ours who serves as a university library director. He jokingly told the students in his Bibliographic Instruction course that it took him over two years to conduct the research needed for his Ph.D. dissertation. Now, with the aid of a few select databases, he could do it in one afternoon with two coffee breaks.

Our experience of the tedium of searching for relevant information has provided us with a strong desire to assist students in gathering information for their research papers, theses, and dissertations. In this chapter we want to acquaint you with a little of the history of some of the most important sources of information while also describing how relevant information can be accessed via special electronic databases.

But some of our students may object: "I'm not engaged in advanced research like a dissertation. Why should I concern myself with information contained in a multitude of indexes and abstracts?" Others appear to be content with only two or three of the latest journal articles. They are happy to skim the surface of a subject in the mistaken belief that once they have received their degree they have also received an education.

By way of response, let us say that being able to interact with the thinking of the finest intellects of this or any other age is a privilege that we should not take lightly. We may not agree with all that these writers have to say, but if we are to make any advances for the cause of Christ in our generation, we must be aware of their contribution. Information literacy (as we explained in the Introduction) is learning how to use different resources so that the quality of the work we do will tend toward excellence.

There's also a bonus to learning about a few basic resource tools. Your own research time will be reduced considerably. Indexes and abstracts are designed to spare you the exhausting and repetitious task which you otherwise would have to undertake if you were to check the contents of each annual volume of each journal that had a bearing on your research. This point is illustrated for us in the experience of an undergraduate pre-law student named Allan. In his last semester he was required to write a *major* term paper on the topic of "Search and Seizure and the Fourth Amendment." It was to be well-documented and replete with citations from recent court cases.

Allan spent a fruitless day going from the library's catalog to the stacks and in the course of twelve hours, checked every book in the library having "Search and seizure" as a subject heading. The result was about as much information as could be rolled up and stuffed into a pitted olive without the scroll protruding from either end.

When we discussed his dilemma the next day, we decided that anything germane to his topic would more likely be found in journal articles. We consulted a law index, and in a few minutes had traced over 200 articles—more than enough to justify the research requirements of his course. Allan then went to a nearby law library and spent the rest of the day photocopying the most important articles so that the information could be taken to his apartment without the need for him to commute back and forth to a law library. With these articles before him, he could mark the stages in the development of the Search and Seizure Law and highlight the sections he wanted to quote in his paper.

The point we wish to make is this: The amount of time Allan spent consulting the index and identifying some of the more relevant articles was reduced to minutes rather than hours. Locating and copying the articles took longer. At no time, however, did he expend his efforts in a vain search for information.

A knowledge of indexes and their use, regardless of whether one is engaged in undergraduate or graduate studies, greatly reduces the tedium of searching for information.

DEFINITIONS

The *Random House Dictionary* defines an index as a "more or less detailed alphabetical listing of names, places, and topics along with the numbers of the pages on which they are mentioned or discussed ...." This is the kind of index with which most of us are familiar. It appears in the back of a book or set of books and directs us to places where we are likely to find the information we need.

Specialized indexes, however, are different. They deal with a general topic, e.g., "Religion," "Medicine," "Health and fitness," or "Humanities." Then, in an *alphabetically arranged subject index*, they list those journal articles or essays that pertain to the topic. Usually the index covers a set period of time and, in the case of most modern ones, is published either annually or biennially.

An abstract is similar to an index. It, too, lists articles and essays under specific subject headings. The basic difference is that a work like *Religious and Theological Abstracts* provides a brief summary of the article or essay. This synopsis is designed to help you determine whether the article in question is sufficiently relevant to your research to be worth locating.

IMPORTANT RESOURCE TOOLS

Our discussion of important indexes and abstracts begins with the following:

Religion Index One: Periodicals

Religion Index Two: Multiple Authors

Biblica/Elenchus Bibliographicus Biblicus/Elenchus of Biblica

Religious and Theological Abstracts

New Testament Abstracts

Old Testament Abstracts

Ephemerides Theologicae Lovanienses

Christian Periodical Index

Catholic Periodical and Literature Index

Index to Jewish Periodical Literature

Internationale Zeitschriftenschau fur Bibelwissenschaft und Grewzgebiete

Religion Index One: Periodicals (1949-present) is a semiannual index with annual cumulations. It has long been regarded as one of the most important resource tools for theological research. The American Theological Library Association (ATLA), publisher of *RIO*, originally published the *Index to Religious Periodical Literature* (1949-1976). The index grew from 31 journals to 58 by 1955-1956, and 203 by 1975-1976. ATLA then revised, expanded, augmented, and renamed *IRPL, Religion Index One: Periodicals*. By 1999 *RIO* was annually indexing more than 12,000 articles in and related to the field of religion from 575 fully and selectively indexed journals and 100 scanned journals.

Articles dealing with aspects of church history, theology, Bible, missions, ministry, philosophy, and religious studies are given a prominent place in *RIO*. Church music, counseling, psychology, and sociology are also represented. Protestant, Catholic, and Jewish journals are included without religious bias. However, a majority of the articles are Protestant.

RIO volumes are divided into three sections: A *Subject Index* which adheres closely to the approved subject headings of the Library of Congress; an *Author Index;* and a *Scripture Index.*

Journal articles on different books of the Bible (or parts of books of the Bible) are arranged under "Bible (O.T.)" or "Bible (N.T.)," as the case may be. To find an article dealing with Paul's thought in Romans 5:12-21, you would need to check the entries in *RIO* under "Bible (N.T.) Romans 5--8." Having located this section, it is a comparatively easy task to find those articles discussing chapter 5. A list of the abbreviations of the names of journals is to be found inside the front cover.

Nearly all denominations are represented in *RIO*. In recent years, however, with the emphasis moving away from organizations and focusing more on people, greater stress seems to have been placed on pastoral and social issues.

Religion Index Two: Multi-Author Works (1960-present) annually indexes essays (chapters in books) from edited or multi-author works, which include *Festschriften*, conference proceedings, congresses, series, and annuals. *RIT* volumes are accessed by searching the *Subject Index, Author and Editor Index*, or the *Scripture Index.*

The *ATLA Religion Database on CD-ROM* provides electronic access to the combined contents of *RIO* and *RIT.* The CD-ROM database also includes *Index to Book Reviews in Religion* (1949-present), *Research in Ministry: An Index to D.Min. Project Reports and Theses* (1981-1998), and *Methodist Reviews Index* (1818-1985). The Standard Search screen allows searching of the entire database through 16 searchable fields, such as keyword, title, author/editor, subject heading, language, and year. The indexes for each field are available for browsing. Boolean searching of the database may be facilitated by using more than one searchable field at a time. Subject headings can also be found in the printed *Religion Indexes: Thesaurus* (1994). Internet access to the ATLA Religion Database is available through FirstSearch, SilverPlatter, Ovid, and EBSCO.

Three subsets of the *ATLA Religion Database* are available on CD-ROM: These are the Ten Year Subset, the Biblical Studies Subset, and the Latin American Subset.

Ethics Index on CD-ROM (1990-1996), which has no print version, was discontinued due to a low subscription rate, but provides access to a wealth of scholarly citations for researchers during this period.

Biblica-->Elenchus Bibliographicus Biblicus-->Elenchus of Biblica (1919-present) form a continuous bibliography. *Biblica*, from 1919 to 1964, was an annual published by the Pontifical Biblical Institute in Rome. It covers journal articles and bibliographies devoted to the books of the Bible; its authority, revelation, and inspiration; canonicity; interpretation; texts and versions; and much more. Each volume indexed about 4,500 articles taken from about 1,500 different journals. And each volume is replete with an index to discussions of Greek and Hebrew words. The articles are in a variety of languages (including German, French, Italian, Spanish, Dutch, and English). Divisions of the index are in Latin, but it does not take a genius to realize that "Archaelogia biblical" is "Biblical archaeology," "Bibliographia" is "Bibliography" and "Textus et vers." is "Texts and Versions," et cetera. An alphabetic index to authors, titles, and subjects makes *Biblica* easy to use.

Between 1968 and 1984 the title was changed from *Biblica* to *Elenchus Bibliographicus Biblicus*. (*Elenchus Bibliographicus* = Biblical record). The articles indexed in each issue now fluctuated between 8,800 and 10,000 per year. Appendices covering archaeological "digs" became extensive, as did reviews of books covering all aspects of archaeology. Special attention was given trade routes, ethnography, and commerce. Attention also focused on exegesis and the writings of the Greek and Latin Fathers; the Reformation; and other theological themes bringing the coverage up to the present time. In addition to the author, title, and subject index, there was added a Scripture index.

In 1985 the name was again changed, this time to *Elenchus of Biblica*. The contents was reformatted, thus making it easier to trace exactly where articles and reviews on a particular subject (e.g., "Textual criticism"; "Psalmorum textus," "Introductio NT," "Hermeneut," or "1-2 Petri") are found.

This index is of greatest importance to doctoral students. While the coverage is excellent, and very few biases are evident, the main drawback of *Elenchus of Biblica* is the time lag between the publication of the journal articles and the appearance of these indices. At present it is about 3 years.

Religious and Theological Abstracts (1958-present) is published quarterly. This non-sectarian abstracting service covers about 378 primarily English-language journals and arranges the material under four broad divisions: Biblical, Theological, Historical, and Practical. Each of these divisions is further subdivided (e.g., "Practical" contains sections on ministry, worship, education, mission, religion and culture, and sociology).

RTA has consistently provided researchers with a variety of information drawn from fields as varied as archaeology and Christian education, philology and contemporary theology, evangelism and church management, apologetics and cross-cultural anthropology, mysticism and the application of ethics to life. What it lacks in quantity it attempts to make up for in quality. *RTA* indexes about 80 journals that are not indexed in *RIO*, and it provides abstracts for all articles.

Quarterly volumes contain Subject and Author indexes. The fourth volume each year includes cumulative Subject, Author, and Scripture indexes, and provides a listing of journals with their addresses. *RTA* on CD-ROM is published annually.

New Testament Abstracts (1956-present) is published three times a year with an annual index of principal Scripture passages covered in the various articles, and separate indices of authors, book reviews and book notices. This abstracting service currently covers approximately 400 scholarly journals dealing with the various areas of New Testament study.

The product of Roman Catholic scholarship, *NTA* is generally unbiased, is international in its scope, and provides critiques in English of articles written in other languages. A CD-ROM version was first published in 1999.

Cumulative indexes are published at regular intervals. All things considered, this is a valuable supplement to the bibliographies published by B. M. Metzger, A. J. and M. B. Mattill, and W. E. Mills (to be discussed in chapter 12) entitled an *Index to Periodical Literature on Christ and the Gospels, Index to Periodical Literature on the Apostle Paul, A Classified Bibliography of Literature on the Acts of the Apostles*, and *A Bibliography of the Periodical Literature on the Acts of the Apostles*, 1962-1984—all of which will aid you in your study of the historic portions of the New Testament.

Old Testament Abstracts (1978-present), also published three times a year, is likewise unbiased. It regularly directs those interested in Old Testament research to journal articles covering everything from "The Ancient Near East: History, Texts, etc." through critical studies on select passages of Scripture to an evaluation of the "Intertestamental, Apocrypha, NT Use." About 330 journals are indexed, and the concise abstract accompanying each entry will be of inestimable value to the researcher using this resource tool.

Book notices are also included in a section following the periodical abstracts. The critique given each book varies from about 600-2,000 words. Indexes to authors, Scripture texts, words in Hebrew and other ancient Languages, and the periodicals abstract are found in the third issue of annual volumes. The Catholic Biblical Association of America, in partnership with ATLA, publishes an annual CD-ROM version of *OTA*.

Ephemerides Theologicae Lovanienses (1924-present) is a resource few people know much about. It is a massive bibliographic tool published by the University of Louvain, Belgium, and it indexes both articles and books, offering a year-end cross-reference index that is most helpful. Its focus is primarily on European works, and in this way it complements *RIO*. At present *Ephemerides* is published irregularly. The major portion, entitled "Elenchus Bibliographicus," provides one of the most complete references to contemporary theological literature available. Material is classified under the following headings: general, historical, religious, Old Testament, New Testament, and theology (with subdivisions in five categories). Numerous English titles are included. An author index, which appears in the final issue each year, completes this handy compilation.

Although recent issues of "Elenchus Bibliographicus" manifest more of an ecumenical approach, researchers will detect a Roman Catholic bias in some of the pre-Vatican II volumes. Works treating the Reformation and contemporary trends within Protestant theology are to be found throughout, although in earlier volumes they appeared under the subject heading "Christianis separatis."

In contrast to *Biblica-->Elenchus Bibliographicus Biblicus-->Elenchus of Biblica*, in which the emphasis was primarily Biblical, *Ephemerides* is of particular value as a theological resource. Its use is hampered by the lack of a proper subject index, and its value is reduced by a lamentable time lag between an article's appearing in print and its inclusion in "Elenchus Bibliographicus." At present this time lag varies between eighteen months and two years.

Christian Periodical Index (1956-present) is issued quarterly with annual cumulations. The index provides researchers with bibliographic citations to evangelical articles in magazines and journals that have not been covered by the other indexing and abstracting agencies. Of the more than 100 titles indexed, about 67 are not covered in *RIO*. The Association of Christian Librarians, which publishes *CPI*, also produces an Internet version.

Catholic Periodical and Literature Index (1967/68-present) is the most current popular index of Roman Catholic publications, and covers more than 190 Catholic periodicals. It serves as the successor to the *Guide to Catholic Literature* (1888-1940) and the *Catholic Periodical Index* (1930-1966). It is published bimonthly with biennial cumulations. *CPLI* is accessed by a subject index, an author and editor index, a book index, and a book review index. The Catholic Library Association and ATLA are publishing an annual CD-ROM version with coverage from 1981 to the present.

Index to Jewish Periodical Literature (1963-present) is an author and subject index to select American and Anglo-Jewish journals of interest to those engaged in the study of (or those who desire a better understanding of) the way in which contemporary Jews view the situation in the Middle East. Included in this index are articles on their feasts, involvement in politics and relief work, together with studies of Biblical texts.

A scholarly work of related interest is *Kiryat Sepher*, published by Jewish National and University Library, Jerusalem. This annotated index (in Hebrew) contains entries relating to published bibliographies, textual studies, Rabbinic literature, philology, and miscellanea.

Last but by no means least, there is the *Internationale Zeitschriftenschau fur Bibelwissenschaft und Grenzgebiete* (1951/52—present). It is devoted to Biblical studies (and particularly Biblical archaeology). Each issue provides researchers with an annual review of journal articles, *Festschriften*, reports, and book reviews in English, German, French, Italian, Spanish, and Dutch, et cetera. In all, about 400 periodicals are indexed. The arrangement is by subject with a "Table of Contents," in German, at the end of each volume. A significant number of the annotations are in English.

LOOKING AHEAD

1. Imagine that you have been placed in charge of the preschool department of your church. What informationcan you find in *Education Abstracts* that will help you (a) understand this age group, (b) minister to their needs, and (c) be able to provide meaningful handcraft materials to occupy their attention.

2. Check the *Family Studies* database and zero in on those areas which deal with the influence of parents (bothfathers and mothers) on their children (sons as well as daughters). What does this indicate about the researchbeing done on dyadic relationships?

12

Specific Reference Tools: Indexes and Abstracts Part 2

When the apostle Paul first wrote the Christians at Thessalonica he concluded his letter with a series of admonitions. Among these parting words of counsel was, *"Prove all things, hold fast to* [that which is] *good"* (1 Thessalonians 5:21).

His instruction was simple; its practice, even today, is difficult. While many rightly believe that God is the Author of all truth, culling the "good" from secular sources requires painstaking care. This has led some to neglect the contribution of others and to rely solely on what the Holy Spirit teaches them. Such sentiments call to mind the wise words of Charles Haddon Spurgeon. When speaking to the students of his Pastor's College, he said:

> ...you are not such wiseacres as to think or say that you can expound Scripture without assistance from the works of divines [i.e., theologians] and learned men who have labored before you .... If you are of that opinion, pray remain so, for you are not worth the trouble of conversion [to a different point of view].... It seems odd, that certain men who talk so much of what the Holy Spirit reveals to themselves, should think so little of what He has revealed to others.... The temptations of our times lie rather in empty pretensions to novelty of sentiment, than in a slavish following of accepted guides. A respectable acquaintance with the opinions of the giants of the past, might have saved many an erratic thinker from wild interpretations and outrageous inferences.[18]

There is much to be gained from the research of others, and the better we know our Bibles, the easier will be the task of discerning and holding fast to that which is good.

Realizing the need for discernment, therefore, and in true submission to the guidance of the Holy Spirit, let us look at areas of theological investigation which can be enriched through the practical application of truth from other related disciplines. In doing so, we will again consider indexes and/or abstracts and focus on the following specific areas of investigation:

- Administration
- Counseling
- Education
- History
- Marriage and the family
- Philosophy
- Sociology and the humanities

Administration

Secular principles for getting things done do not always mesh with the teaching contained in the Word of God. A synthesis, however, can be achieved as is illustrated in two books: *Nehemiah and the Dynamics of Effective Leadership*, and *Leadership: The Dynamics of Success*. True integration of different disciples is difficult, but this does not mean that we should not strive for excellence in this most rewarding of pursuits. Where primacy is given the Scriptures, and secular theories are integrated only where they have been were found to be in harmony with the Biblical text, then much can be gained.

In the administration of the church, and in the training of young people for positions of leadership, in planning ahead and organizing one's time, in leading meetings and working with people in committees, a great deal of helpful information can be found in several online databases such as: *Wilson Business Abstracts*, *ABI/Inform*, or *LEXIS-NEXIS Academic Universe*.

For those who may not have access to these electronic databases, *Business Periodical Index* (1958-present) is the printed index for journals in business. It is published annually and is arranged alphabetically with author and subject entries appearing together. Biographical articles are listed under the name of the biographee. *"See"* references guide the researcher from a term not used as an approved subject heading to one that is; *"See also"* references lead the user from one approved subject heading to another. Approximately 320 professional journals and magazines and trade papers are regularly indexed in *BPI*.

The value of *BPI* and/or these databases to those preparing for, or already in, Christian work, is that they contain a veritable gold mine of information useful for church administration. Topics include insurance, copyright, use of technology, tax law, legal issues, business plans, and marketing. These topics may be interrelated to the ministry of the church or the running of educational institutions or the work of missions as assessing a person's ability, keeping proper records, following efficient administrative practices, understanding the dynamics of decision-making, discerning the principles of executive leadership, perceiving the role of women in administration and management, using wise advertising, developing sound corporate leadership, establishing the lines of communication, and insuring proper development within the community, et cetera.

Students doing research on the administration of a local church will find a wealth of insightful material in any one of these databases. The secular material presented may not always parallel the teaching of the Word of God, and where it differs from the biblical model, reference to these databases will often provide illustrations of those individuals or corporations who adhered to human theories and failed.

Counseling

Few challenges can compare with the ministry of "helps" or "exhortation" or "showing mercy" or the exercise of the gift of "wisdom" and "discernment" in understanding another's problems so that the balm of Scripture can be applied graciously and tactfully to hurting people. And few areas of the pastor's work demand greater understanding and flexibility than counseling. A knowledge of personality is essential, and some awareness of human stages of development, pathology, and different therapeutic skills is also necessary.

When it comes to specifics, however, the issues a pastor may encounter may range all the way from adolescent rebellion to indoctrination by those who espouse Zen-Buddhism, or from alcoholism to withdrawal, states of anxiety to various forms of repression, defense mechanisms to transference, depression to sublimation, escapism to reaction formation, frustration to projection, hostility to negativism, and intellectualization to masochism. The counselor, therefore, soon becomes aware of his or her need for a high level of technical expertise. Then, the question of the moment is, Where can he find a competent discussion of this issue?

Although it may at first seem strange, one of the best sources of scholarly information for counseling is *Index Medicus* (1960-present). *Index Medicus* is cumulated annually as *Cumulated Index Medicus,* and is available electronically in *Medline* (1966-present). *IM/Medline* contains information about articles written by psychiatrists (and a few psychologists). In these articles you will find various modes of counseling discussed together with different approaches to specific problems.

IM/Medline includes extensive Subject and Author indexes. The Subject Index is accessed by MeSH (Medical Subject Headings) which is listed alphabetically on Book 1 of *Cumulated Index Medicus. Medline* allows keyword browsing of titles, abstracts, and MeSH headings.

While many entries in *Medline* deal with medicine and science, psychiatry has long been associated with the medical profession and extensive coverage is given to counseling. Researchers will find scholarly articles on a variety of topics such as the therapeutic treatment of alcoholism, biofeedback, work with terminally ill patients, the diagnosis and treatment of hypertension, family therapy, problems experienced by people in mid-life, or old age (with special consideration being given physiological and psychological aspects of gerontology), the dilemma of abortion, a variety of sexual dysfunctions, the care and rehabilitation of the disabled, candid discussions of homosexuality, and many other topics that can easily be traced through the subject index. In addition, articles written by outstanding physicians such as C. Everett Koop may be traced through the author index.

Another source of information which counselors may find helpful is *Psychological Abstracts* (1927-present). Monthly issues include an Author Index and a Brief Subject Index, which cumulate in the Annual Subject Index and Annual Author Index. Abstracts cover 19 divisions including: Human Experimental Psychology, Social Process & Social Issues, Psychological and Physical Disorders, and Health & Mental Health Treatment & Prevention. Subject headings are based on the terms found in the *Thesaurus of Psychological Index Terms.*

The easiest way to find journal articles through *Psychological Abstracts* is via the electronic versions *PsycINFO* and *PsycLit. PsycINFO* (1887-present) is updated monthly and covers journals, technical reports, dissertations, book chapters, and books. *PsycLit* (1974-present for journals, 1987-present for books) is the CD-ROM version. It is updated quarterly and does not include dissertations or technical reports.

Bibliographic control in psychology is fairly good because, prior to *PA, Psychological Index* (1894-1935) was being published by the Psychological Review Company in Princeton. Some overlap obviously occurred between the years 1927 and 1935, but for all practical purposes, by using both *Psychological Index* and *Psychological Abstracts* the literature from 1894 to the 1960s and 70s, including the writings of authors from Sigmund Freud to Gary Collins can be traced quickly and easily.

There is one glaring weakness to *PA*, however, and it lies in the "selective indexing" of journal articles. Preference is given those journals approved or published by the American Psychological Association, and even with these favoritism seems to be given those articles of an experimental or empirical nature (particularly if they are accompanied by a sophisticated research design).

Education

Not to be ignored by those interested in Christian education are *ERIC* (1966-present) and *Education Abstracts* (1983-present). *ERIC* (*Educational Resources Information Center*) is an electronic database comprised of the monthly *Current Index to Journals in Education* (*CIJE*) and the monthly *Resources in Education* (*RIE*) which indexes nonjournal documents. Published by the Federal Government, the *ERIC* database covers all areas of education including Christian schools and home schooling. A list of useful subject headings for accessing *ERIC* can be found in the *Thesaurus of ERIC Descriptors*.

Education Abstracts is the electronic version of *Education Index* (1929-present). While concentrating attention on preschool, elementary, secondary and higher education, a vast array of material is also to be found on school administration, vocational counseling, teaching methods, curriculum development, the use of multimedia, the importance of the library, and special education. Those involved with Christian day schools as well as those preparing to teach on a graduate level will receive added stimulus for their research from their consultation of *Education Abstracts*. Furthermore, viable work done in the areas of beliefs and values, the interplay between moral development and true maturity, and one's identity through teaching/learning experiences, can all be traced with relative ease.

History

An awareness of the historical setting, in which people lived and moved, can likewise enrich beyond measure your appreciation of what they did. Hiram, king of Tyre built a "house" for King David in Jerusalem. What was it like? How was it furnished? Was it a luxurious and awe-inspiring edifice? Would it have rivaled the palatial munificence of the Borghese Villa in Rome or the splendor of Hampton Court near London?[19] Were the ceramic utensils David used comparable to the workmanship of artisans in Crete or Rhodes who lived during the same period? And if there were differences in ornamentation and design, what were they?

Matters of historical importance impinge on all disciplines. For example, what educational principles did Alcuin use that brought about the Carolingian renaissance? How did the struggle for spiritual and political freedom impact the Huguenots? Why did the Anabaptists prefer martyrdom to renouncing their beliefs? And in more recent times, how has a new awareness of human dignity brought changes to American foreign policy as well as the delegation of responsibility to nationals by many missionary organizations?

There are many important works that are deserving of your attention. Two of these are *Historical Abstracts: Bibliography of the World's Periodical Literature* (1955-present) and *America: History and Life* (1964-present).

Historical Abstracts (1955-present) provides brief summations of the contents of journal articles, books, and dissertations. Over 2,100 journals from 90 countries and about 40 languages are abstracted. The material is arranged by subject, topic, and "Area of Country" of the world. Missiologists should not ignore the up-to-date data on the peoples and places of special interest to them or their mission. Historical theologians will find abstracts to articles on people and movements in church history.

Issued quarterly in two parts with annual cumulations, *Historical Abstracts* deals with Modern History, 1450-1914 (Part A), and Twentieth Century History (Part B). The arrangement in each volume is by topic with further subdivisions and subject refinement. Bibliographical articles on a particular country or area are placed within the appropriate geographic division. Within each division the sequence is alphabetical by author. A subject index, an author index, and a list of periodicals concludes each volume.

America: History and Life (1964-present) provides access to more than 2,100 American and foreign journals, in addition to films, video recordings, books, and dissertations. Focused mainly on the history and culture of Canada and the United States, *America* is a fruitful source of information on the history of American religious leaders and groups.

Historical Abstracts and *America: History and Life* can be accessed via CD-ROM or the Internet. Features of the CD-ROM (DOS) version are similar to the *ATLA Religion Database*.

Marriage and the Family

Of great importance in the life of the church and the nation is the family. Changes, however, are taking place with great rapidity. The "nuclear family" of the 1960s has now given way to "dual career families" and "single parent families" with "latch-key kids" and a variety of other phenomena unknown a generation or two ago. And who can predict what lies in store in the future?

Literature on marriage and the family has assumed "Himalayan" proportions. As formidable as it appears, it can easily be reduced to manageable size by using the following resource tools.

The International Bibliography of Research in Marriage and the Family, 1900-1964, edited by J. Aldous and R. Hill (1967) was designed to cover six and a half crucial decades and bring before researchers as much of the salient literature on marriage and the family as possible. This compilation of articles helps those studying the dynamics of family relationships review a wealth of historical material to determine if any of it is relevant to their present studies. Sufficient to say that with the publication of this volume the editors made available a resource tool that facilitated high quality research.

A change of title occurred with the publication of volume 3, and with this change the editorial "mantle" fell upon the shoulders of new editors led by David Olson of the Family Social Science Department of the University of Minnesota. Now called *The Inventory of Marriage and Family Literature* (1973—1992), this annual cumulation indexed the most important material published on marriage and the family. The final print volumes were edited by John Touliatos and published by the National Council on Family Relations.

In 1996 the printed volumes were superseded by the *Family Studies Database* (1970-present) on CD-ROM or the Internet. This electronic database indexes aver 1,000 journals, books, and other marriage and family resources.

Not all journals are fully indexed, with the result that excellent biblical and/or theological approaches to marriage and the family must be traced through other sources. Evangelical users of *Family Studies Database* will find that its contents is weak in coverage of authors such as James Dobson, Gary Collins, Norm Wright, or Larry Crabb. However, all things considered, this database stands as the finest subject index for the study of marriage and family available today.

In addition to the *Family Studies Database*, information will also be found in the *Child Development Abstracts and Bibliography* (1927-present). It regularly indexes about 275 professional journals, important books, and other materials covering the research literature on the development of children. The arrangement of *CDAB* is by topic with each entry assigned a number. Browsing through an issue should spark off ideas for a score of research papers where secular research is illuminated by the teaching of Scripture. Cumulated Author and Subject indexes conclude each annual volume.

Philosophy

For comprehensive coverage of philosophy books and journals in English, French, German, Spanish, and Italian along with selected books and journals in other languages and related disciplinary publications, there is nothing to equal the *Philosopher's Index* (1967-present). Published quarterly with annual cumulations, this index provides researchers with access to information contained in approximately 300 journals. The arrangement of the index is by subject (with extensive sections on God, religion, truth, and ethics, etc.), by an author index with abstracts, and by a book review index. The *Philosopher's Index* on CD-ROM or the Internet provides retrospective searching of books and journals from 1940 to the present.

Humanities and Social Sciences Indexes

Of considerable value to those engaged in applying theological truths to life are the *Humanities Index* (1974-present) and the *Social Sciences Index* (1974-present). Both publications are issued quarterly with annual cumulations, and they both are indexed by subject followed by a section of book reviews. Their CD-ROM or Internet versions are *Humanities Abstracts* (1984-present) and *Social Sciences Abstracts* (1983-present), and most of the contents of both are covered in large online databases such as *Expanded Academic ASAP*, *ProQuest Research Library*, or *Academic Search Elite*.

Humanities Index (indexing more than 300 titles) abounds with references to subjects in and related to religion and religious life. Numerous "See also" references lead the researcher to citations in subjects such as: God, faith, missions, theology, and worship. *Social Sciences Index* (indexing more than 350 titles) contains less in the area of religion but provides more in the areas of family studies, social work, gerontology, women's studies, minority studies, moral development, and anthropology. An abundance of articles can be found in the areas of parenting, child/children, mothers, et cetera. Stress in both indexes is laid primarily upon American history, literature and culture, and, in this connection, the student of social mores in the United States will find a wealth of material to occupy his or her time.

Of a different genre is *PAIS International in Print* (1991-present) from Public Affairs Information Service. Issued monthly with quarterly cumulations and an annual cumulation, *PAIS* is of value to theologians, pastors, and missionaries for its international studies, statistics, information on developing countries, education, family life, different kinds of impingements upon human freedom, the growth of various religions and cults, information about a variety of professions, the study of different age groups, data about women's rights, and details about minorities. While often ignored by those in Christian circles, *PAIS* is freighted with usable material.

PAIS annually scans approximately 1,600 journals and 8,000 books. It is also available in CD-ROM versions (1972-present) and through several Internet services.

A work of related significance is *Sociological Abstracts* (1952-present), which is published in seven times a year with annual cumulative index. *SA* indexes add abstracts journal articles under 29 topics including: social psychology, group interactions, sociology of religion, the family and socialization, studies in poverty, et cetera. Subject, author, and source indexes enhance its usefulness. Access to information in *SA* is more easily obtained through various Internet or CD-ROM versions such as *Sociofile* (1974-present).

LOOKING AHEAD

Take a topic of your own choosing. By consulting the *Library of Congress Subject Headings* ascertain the approved headings under which material is likely to be found. Now check the last five years of *Bibliographic Index*, using each of the headings you have uncovered through the *L. C. Subject Headings*. Make a note of the entries and then try to locate some of the books or journals referred to in *Bibliographic Index*. How extensive is each author's bibliography? If you were doing advanced research, how valuable to you would the data collected *via* these select bibliographies?

13

Bibliographies
Part 1

It has become popular today for liberals in both politics and education to try and rewrite history. Biases have already been included in textbooks with the result that entire generations of students are growing to adulthood with a purposefully skewed view of the past. And politicians, aided by the media, believe that if they distort the truth often enough people will come to accept what they tell them. All of this highlights the importance of possessing an acute awareness of what has taken place in the past. Because many indexes and abstracts only selectively index journals, and many students concentrate on what has been written over the last five-to-ten years, it is necessary for each of us to diligently search for truth and be aware of resources that include retrospective materials as well as past events and accomplishments.

The task facing each one of us is an exacting one that requires considerable perseverance. So, even though databases have made searching much easier, you need to be aware of sources of information that will enable you to move beyond the "latest research" and the "most current data." This is particularly true in Biblical studies and theology. *Truth is timeless.* Whereas research in the arts and sciences dates quickly, the opposite is often true in Biblical studies and theology. That which is old is often preferable to what in time will be shown to be just another current fad.

GENERAL BIBLIOGRAPHIES

The *Bibliographic Index: A Cumulative Bibliography of Bibliographies* (1938-present) is a compilation of bibliographies that have been published separately in books or journal articles. It regularly examines approximately 2,600 periodicals for substantial bibliographies and selects those that contain at least 50 citations. These citations include materials from English, as well as the Germanic and Romance Languages. *BI* has been published semiannually since 1965, with annual cumulations, is the product of many people and makes available to the researcher a vast amount of viable material that might otherwise escape his or her attention. *BI* is not available online.

The arrangement of *BI* is alphabetical by subject only. Under each subject heading entries are arranged alphabetically by author. All subjects are covered, and each annual volume can lead you to secular as well as religious sources of information on a seemingly innumerable array of topics.

SPECIAL BIBLIOGRAPHIES

As the focus of one's research narrows, specific attention may need to focus on the:

• Bible

• Church history and the study of comparative religions

• Missions and ecumenics

• Pastoral theology

The works mentioned under each of these headings will be representative of the vast reservoir of material to which new works are continuously being added.

Bible

Most theological databases place relatively little emphasis on the Bible, and so we will try to counteract this neglect by dealing with some sources of information that you may find helpful.

A popular work, rich in resources from the period of the Puritans to the 19th century, is Charles Haddon Spurgeon's *Commenting and Commentaries* (1876/1989). It contains 1437 entries covering works treating the entire Bible (or portions of the Bible), as well as commentaries devoted to individual books of the Bible. Each entry is annotated, and the books that Spurgeon highly recommended are printed in heavy type.

Another work devoted exclusively to Bible commentaries is James E. Rosscup's *Commentaries for Biblical Expositors* (1993). Rosscup divides commentaries into three divisions: Detailed exegetical, expositional survey, and devotional flavor. His work is annotated and reliable, exceedingly helpful, and replaces any former reliance one may have had on Brevard S. Childs' *Old Testament Books for Pastor and Teacher* (1977) and Ralph P. Martin's *New Testament Books for Pastor and Teacher* (1984).

Also of value, and listing publications printed from the late 19th-century to the present, is *The Minister's Library*. Though *TML* includes chapters devoted to theology, devotional literature, church history, Christian education, and comparative religions, its primary emphasis is on Bible commentaries of interest to the pastor. *TML* is ongoing and up-to-date. Each entry is annotated.

Old Testament

Where the study of the Old Testament is concerned, the Society for Old Testament Study (SOTS) has regularly issued a *Book List* (1945-present). Its purpose is to keep scholars appraised of the latest publications in a variety of areas related to the study of the Old Testament. Though English titles predominate, a sizeable number of entries are in foreign languages (e.g., German, French, Spanish, Italian, et cetera).

Among the other volumes published by SOTS are H. H. Rowley's *Eleven Years of Bible Bibliography* (1957), B. W. Anderson's *A Decade of Bible Bibliography* (1967), and P. R. Ackroyd's *Bible Bibliography, 1967-1973, Old Testament* (1974). Each entry is accompanied by a scholarly critique. Combined, these books are a most valuable asset in the hands of the researcher.

A retrospective resource of great value is the University of Chicago's *Catalog of the Oriental Institute Library* (16 vols.; 1970) which alerts users to more than 50,000 items dealing with the art, literature, philology, history, science and religious beliefs of those living in the countries comprising the ancient Near East. A supplementary *Catalog of the Middle Eastern Collection* was issued in 1977.

And then there is William G. Hupper's *An Index to English Periodical Literature on the Old Testament and Ancient Near East* (1987-). At the present time six volumes have made their appearance. Hupper's "Herculean" efforts have focused on more than 600 journals covering such allied fields as archaeology, history, philology, science, and theology. The coverage in the volumes available thus far is from 1793 to 1969-70. This is a massive work with the material arranged in chronological order under within specific sections. Informative data can be gathered on Old Testament personalities, the history of Israel, the usage of different words, the sociology and culture of the people, women in society, agriculture, metallurgy, warfare, commerce and economics, monetary systems, and much more.

No survey of the literature of the Old Testament would be complete without some information on the Septuagint. In this connection the *Classified Bibliography to the Septuagint*, compiled by S. P. Brock, C. T.

Fritzsch and S. Jellicoe (1973) fills a real need. It covers the period from 1860 to 1969, and evidences great care in the selection of materials for inclusion. In all, the compilers consulted nearly 200 sources, and arranged the entries culled from these journals and scholarly monographs under specific subject headings. A comprehensive table of contents and index of authors indicates where the data was found. Material published after 1969 can be traced through *Religion Index One (RIO)*.

Students should not neglect *Old Testament Abstracts*, and as other works of a similar nature are being issued, the wise student will pay close attention to his or her school's library acquisition list so as to know when new volumes are added to the collection.

New Testament

As we consider the New Testament, we find numerous indexes awaiting our attention. Bruce M. Metzger is to be complimented on being the prime mover behind the compilation of the *Index to Periodical Literature on Christ and the Gospels* (1966) and the *Index to Periodical Literature on the Apostle Paul* (1970). Both are part of the New Testament Tools and Studies series.

As near complete as possible, the *Index to Periodical Literature on Christ and the Gospels* brings before the user a wealth of scholarly resource material taken from 160 periodicals published in 16 languages. While recourse can always be made to *New Testament Abstracts* and *RIO*, the value of Metzger's work is that it makes available information contained in journals published during the last century and the first half of this century. The format includes a detailed table of contents as well as helpful indexes.

A companion volume, the *Index to Periodical Literature on the Apostle Paul*, provides access to a vast storehouse of literature drawn from more than 100 scholarly journals. The entries are arranged alphabetically by author under a comprehensive list of subjects and cover historical, philological, theological and ecclesiastical aspects of Paul's life and ministry.

First published in 1960, this retrospective bibliographic index supplements the information in *RIO*, for it concentrates on essays written during the 19th century and the first five decades of this century. An author index is included.

Serving as a companion volume to the works by B. M. Metzger is the *Classified Bibliography of Literature on the Acts of the Apostles* by A. J. and M. B. Mattill. This well-indexed, 6,646-entry bibliography contains references to essays from 180 periodicals in all the major European languages. Beginning with "Bibliographical Studies," the researcher is introduced to a mind-boggling array of data among which are articles on textual criticism; philology; literary criticism; history; the theology of the early church and its leaders; character studies; chronology; archaeology; Roman laws, customs, and institutions; pseudepigraphal literature; et cetera. Preachers, researchers and professors can all benefit from its use.

The work by Mattill and Mattill has been brought up-to-date by Watson E. Mills who issued his *Bibliography of the Periodical Literature on the Acts of the Apostles, 1962-1984* in 1986. The material in this index is arranged alphabetically. The indexing to the periodical literature is impressive, and Mills succeeds in placing at a student's fingertips a wealth of important data.

Church History

General Reference Works

Scripture, of course, is designed to form the basis of religious belief. The study of church history and the different religions that have arisen reveals that this basic principle has not been followed. The "seed of the Word" has been sown, but there has also been a counter-sowing of "darnel" (cf. Matthew 13:24-30). Church history and a study of comparative religions, therefore, needs to be seen in light of the emergence of these different ideologies and the movements that have grown up about them. These various teachings need to be diligently compared to the teaching of the Bible and, inasmuch as history forms the backdrop for this kind of study, historical sources must, of necessity, be included if one's research into any facet of religious belief or practice is to have validity.

The bibliographies referred to in this section are representative of the many that are available at the present time. Additional information can be obtained from James E. Bradley and Richard A. Muller's *Church History: An Introduction to Research, Reference Works, and Methods* (1995). It provides thorough coverage of the different eras and facets of history. The product of a collaborative effort on the part of church historians, historians, systematic theologians, librarians makes this work indispensable. The detailed organization of the book is found in the "Contents," and under each heading or subheading there is such an abundance of information as to meet the needs of most researchers all the way through to their doctoral studies.

Early Christianity

Of a more specialized nature is Bruce M. Metzger's *Index of Articles on the New Testament and the Early Church Published in Festschriften*

(1951), to which a Supplement was added in 1955. This work succeeds in directing the scholar to a vast storehouse of easily overlooked data. The bibliographies at the end of these essays are very full and cannot help but increase the reservoir of material from which one may do his or her research.

Also of value in the study of the early church is *Bibliographia Patristica: Internationale Patristische Bibliographies,* edited by W. Schallmelcher (1959-present). Published annually, this detailed index to the literature and religion, symbols and doctrine, people and practice of the period of the Church Fathers, provides the user with access to information contained in about 900 scholarly journals in a variety of European languages guide to historical literature--from periodical and newspaper articles, books and book reviews, dissertations and encyclopedic articles--provides excellent coverage of the ancient and medieval periods.

History of Religions/Medieval History

Of a different nature is the *International Bibliography of the History of Religions,* edited by S. H. Alich (1974-present). It furnishes researchers with information about all the major religions of the Near East.

When it comes to the Medieval period, the *Dictionary Catalog of the Library of the Pontifical Institute of Medieval Studies* of St. Michael's College, Toronto (5 vols. and Supplement; 1972) provides investigators with access to a variety of source materials dealing with everything from religious ritual to religious paintings, from sacred music to the copying and preserving of sacred manuscripts, from court intrigue to Byzantine customs, from canon law to civil practice, and from vernacular literature to Bible translations.

British History

The propagation of the gospel in England is chronicled in a series of bibliographies. The first, a *Bibliography of British History; Tudor Period, 1485-1603,* edited by C. Read (1959), was published in 1963. Arranged under broad topics (e.g., political history, ecclesiastical history), it provides excellent coverage of the literature of the period. Some of the entries are annotated. This work is a must for students of the reformation and the era that gave rise to the Puritans and the early non-conformists.

Likewise, the *Bibliography of British History; Stuart Period, 1603-1714,* edited by G. Davies and M. F. Keeler (1970), continues the admirable coverage provided in the earlier volume. In many instances, the annotations are longer, and this work includes sections on the Puritans, Anglican and Presbyterian churches during this period, and the place and influence of Jews in England during the 17th century.

Continuing coverage is contained in the *Bibliography of British History; the Eighteenth Century, 1714-1789*, edited by S. M. Pargellis and D. J. Medley (1951). This bibliography is well outlined and treats the Nonconformist movement in England. It also provides indispensable coverage of the material relating to social conditions in England (and elsewhere) during the time of Wesley and Whitefield.

Also of value is the *Bibliography of British History, 1789-1851*, edited by L. M. Brown and I. R. Christie (1977), which is replete with introductory essays, a chronicle of the expansion of the British empire (including Captain James Cook who opened up the way for missionaries to evangelize each of the islands and countries he visited). Also to be found within these covers is information on the expansion of the British Empire and the rise and progress of missions.

Coverage continues with the *Bibliography of British History, 1851-1914*, compiled and edited by H. J. Hanham (1976). This mammoth volume carries forward the growth of the British Empire and, as the contents plainly show, deals primarily with England's era of power and influence. Interesting sections treat progress in industry, education and the social sciences.

Finally, there is *A Bibliography of British History, 1914—1989,* edited by Keith Robbins (1996). It covers both world wars as well as the religious and social problems people in the United Kingdom have faced.

With these volumes so readily available, no student should believe that he or she is bereft of resources when asked to write on any facet of British history.

American History

Turning now to American history, few works can compare with the *Guide to the Study of the United States of America*, published by the General Reference and Bibliographic Division of the Library of Congress (1960, with supplements from 1976-), and the *Harvard Guide to American History*, by F. B. Freidel and R. K. Showman (Revised ed.; 1974/ 1980). The former annotates most entries and provides a single author-title-subject index. The latter, following a series of introductory essays, helps researchers zero in on bibliographical data and personal records, specific areas of interest (e.g., interpretative accounts of American history), as well as regional, state and local histories, special subjects [government, lay, politics, economics, education, etc.], and a plethora of other topics. In all, more than 400 journals are indexed, making this a valuable resource.

Trends in history can also be traced through the American Historical Association's *Guide to Historical Literature*, edited by C. F. Howe, et al

(1961/1970). This comprehensive, annotated guide to historical litera-ture—from periodical and newspaper articles, books and book reviews, dissertations and encyclopedia articles—provides excellent coverage of the ancient and medieval periods.

Missions and Ecumenics

Closely associated with the ministry of the church is the whole area of missions. Whereas formerly missionaries did the work of evangelism, today much more is required of them. A study of the culture of the people with which one will be working, together with an understanding of their history and beliefs, their method of socialization and leadership, economic practices and outlook on the future, are indispensable to a missionary's preparation.

One of the most comprehensive collections of materials on Protes-tant missions was accumulated by the Missionary Research Library in New York. Bearing the title *Dictionary Catalog of the Missionary Re-search Library* (17 vols.; 1968), this outstanding index to books has been located since 1929 on the campus of the Union Theological Seminary, New York. The catalog contains more than 100,000 entries and has au-thor, title and subject indexes.

The Library of Congress, Africa Section, has published *Africa South of the Sahara: Index to Periodical Literature, 1900-1970* (4 vols.; 1971), which makes accessible a vast amount of information on topics like eth-nography, sociology, linguistics and politics of all nations on the African continent. This work is a *must* for the student of missions.

Other related works include the *Cumulative Bibliography of African Studies*, published by the International African Institute, London (5 vols.; 1973). Information is grouped under geographic areas, with subdivisions by subject, people and language.

And then there is *The Howard University Bibliography of African and Afro-American Religious Studies*, prepared by Ethel L. Williams and C. F. Brown (1977) which provides access to about 13,000 primary and secondary sources. A helpful feature is the listing of approximately 230 American libraries where the information contained in this bibliography may be found.

The University of California, Berkeley, has published their *East Asia Library: Author-Title Catalog* (23 vols.; 1968) by means of which they enable students of linguistics and Asian culture to have access to one of the largest collections of Chinese, Japanese and Korean materials ever assembled. In addition, these volumes are filled with information relat-ing to the religions of these peoples and communistic influence in these countries.

A work of related significance is the *Cumulative Bibliography of Asian Studies, 1941-1965* (8 vols.; 1965) with well over 100,000 entries, and the 1966-1970 Supplement (6 vols.; 1972-1973) of approximately 70,000 additional entries. These latter volumes have extensive sections devoted to Vietnam and Indochina.

Of a similar nature is the *Catalog of the Latin American Library of the Tulane University Library* in New Orleans (9 vols.; 1970), with supplements appearing every two years. This outstanding Latin American library was known until 1962 as the Middle American Research Institute Library. It was started in 1924 with the purchase of the William Gates Collection, comprising materials on Mexico, Central America and the West Indies. Other private collections have since been added, and the *Catalog* now includes material for all of Latin America, most of which deals with the social sciences and humanities.

The *Catalog* is arranged in dictionary form but generally does not contain entries for newspapers, manuscripts or maps, although main entries for Latin American materials now found in other divisions of the Tulane University Library are included.

Also of value is the *Index to Latin American Periodical Literature, 1929-1960* (8 vols.; 1962), and the 1961-1965 Supplement. With preference given matters of cultural, economic, educational, historical, political, and social importance, this work can be of estimable value to the D.Miss. candidate interested in the cross-cultural communication of the Gospel.

Finally, *Protestantism in Latin America: A Bibliographic Guide*, edited by J. H. Sinclair (1976), is a "made-for-missionaries" bibliography which includes resource and study tools, provides an introduction to sources of information on the customs and culture, and describes the history of those who have labored there for Christ since the first missions were established.

Bibliographies of the leading religions are legion. Two will suffice to illustrate the kind of works that are available: (1) *Studies of Chinese Religion: A Comprehensive and Classified Bibliography of Publications in English, French and German Through 1970*, compiled by L. G. Thompson (1976), contains entries arranged under 82 subject headings. The entries are not annotated; an author index is provided. And (2) *Index Islamicus, 1906-1955*, compiled by J. D. Pearson (1958), is a basic resource for the study of Islamic history and religion, ideology and culture. Information is gleaned from about 510 periodicals, 120 *Festschriften* and more than 70 other works. It is kept up to date with quinquennial indexes to current literature.

Some missiologists will be interested in the Ecumenical Movement and the library holdings and publications of the World Council of Churches, Geneva. The following are a few of the works they may wish to consult.

The World Council of Churches published a *Classified Catalog of the Ecumenical Movement* (2vols.; 1972) listing approximately 52,000 books and pamphlets, 1,350 periodicals of which 750 are current,and 6,500 boxes of archival materials. The ecumenical sections contain approximately 11,000 titles that are indexed in the Classified Catalog, arranged according to a modified Dewey Decimal system. The collection consists of the history of various ecumenical movements in the 20th century, the history of the World Council of Churches, all reports and publications of its divisions, departments, et cetera, since 1948, complete records of the four WCC Assemblies, records of World Confessional Families, publications of national and regional councils of churches, The Library of the World Council of Churches published a *Classified Catalog of the Ecumenical Movement* church union negotiations and surveys, Vatican II and non-Catholic reactions, all aspects of ecumenical theology (ecumenical literature is also included), and ecumenical biographies.

Other works of related significance include the brief but informative compilation by Paul A. Crow, Jr., *The Ecumenical Movement in Bibliographical Outline* (1965); and *Laici in ecclesia* (1961), both of which list books and other materials on the role of the laity in the life and mission of the church. And then there is the *Internationale Oekumenische Bibliographic. International Ecumenical Bibliography. Bibliographic Oecumenique Internationale. Bibliografie Ecumenica International* (1967-present), an annual which, as the title suggests, is published in German, English, French and Italian, and is one of the most comprehensive, continuous, classified bibliographies available. It is designed to keep researchers appraised of the literature in the field.

Other bibliographic guides of interest to missionaries have been released by G. K. Hall and Company, Boston, and Scarecrow Press, Metuchen, NJ. These guides are easy to use, cover nearly every corner of the earth, have more than one million new items of information added to them annually, and the material can be accessed by either author, title, or subject.

In our next chapter we will consider bibliographies in the applied areas of pastoral theology.

LOOKING AHEAD

What are congregations looking for in a pastor? Make a list of the skills and attributes most commonly sought for by pulpit committees.

Arrange the entries in their order of importance. Assuming that you are working on a graduate degree in this area, how would you go about gathering data about the church's pastoral needs? Prepare a brief bibliography on one of these areas: homiletics, pastoral administration/leadership, the Christian education program, or counseling.

14

Bibliographies
Part 2

PASTORAL THEOLOGY

What do churches look for when choosing a new pastor? A list of the criteria might surprise (and disappoint) you. Depending on the make up of the search committee, you might find stress being placed on a pastor being able to "get things done," or be a "people person," or be a good manager, able to teach people of all ages, have the skills of an artist or a diplomat, be a powerful speaker, a master of ceremonies, a wise counselor—and only incidentally be a man of the Word who is sensitive to the leading of the Holy Spirit.

Quite apart from the unrealistic expectations of church boards, it is only after being in the ministry for some time that you will be able to measure up to the multi-faceted requirements of a pastorate.

In this chapter we will focus on bibliographic research in the following areas:

• The development of pastoral skills

• The ministry of music

• The ministry of education

• Ministry to ethnic groups

• The ministry of counseling

Each of these areas is wide open for research, particularly on the part of those pursuing D.Min. degrees.

The Development of Pastoral Skills

In addition to a mastery of Bible and theology and some proficiency in the original languages, pastors also need to have a knowledge of their own personality dynamics (their strengths and weaknesses). Here are a few resources, written or compiled by specialists that may be of help to an aspiring pastor.

Homiletics. First, there is *Recent Homiletic Thought: A Bibliography, 1935-1965*, edited by W. Toohey and W. D. Thompson (1967). It begins with the year in which C. H. Dodd gave his lectures on "The Apostolic Preaching and Its Developments" at King's College, London, and then surveys ten different areas of the preacher's role, concluding with a bibliography. Each entry is annotated. A comprehensive list of theses and dissertations in the area of sermon preparation and delivery concludes the work. Interdenominational in scope, this compilation of materials is ecumenical in its content and coverage.

Volume 2, bearing the same title, covers the years from 1966-1979. It was edited by A. D. Litfin and H. W. Robinson. The format is the same as the earlier edition, and the coverage is excellent.

With many churches expanding their ministries to include audio and visual means of sharing the Gospel, *Communication: A Guide to Information Sources* by George Gitter and R. Grunin (1980) provides excellent coverage for the study of mass media and cross-cultural communication, with special emphasis being placed on motivation, the use of television and different aspects of journalism.

Also of vital importance to pastors is leadership. For many years people have relied on Ralph M. Stogdill's *Leadership Abstracts and Bibliography, 1904-1974* (1977). This annotated bibliography to more than 3,000 books and journal articles directed researchers to professional materials and made available a vast resource of empirically verified data. It is well indexed and ideal for those studying leadership dynamics. This work is now dated and has value only as it records the work of others noting their differing hypotheses, tests, and presenting their results.

Some of these concepts have been applied to managerial leadership, and these are found in Bernard M. Bass and Ralph M. Stogdill's *Handbook of Leadership: Theory, Research, and Managerial Application*, (3d ed.; 1990). It is one of the most important secular resources extant, for it reviews 5,000 works on leadership theory and research, including managerial styles, and methods of training. It includes author and subject indexes.

The Ministry of Music

Though many still rely on John Julian's massive work *A Dictionary of Hymnology* (2 vols.; 1907/1985), covering Christian hymns of all ages, a vast amount of information can also be obtained from the *Judson Con-*

cordance to Hymns by T. B. McDormans and F. S. Crossman. Today, however, the most useful sources of information are *Music Index* and the *Repertoire Internationale de la Litterature Musicale (RILM)* located in *FirstSearch.* It contains over 200,000 citations on international music and corresponds to the printed RILM Abstracts of Music Literature.

The *Music Index* (1949-present) indexes by author and title about 350 periodicals worldwide. Some of the journals are indexed selectively. All aspects of music are included, including obituaries, book reviews, reviews of performances and recordings. The main problem with the printed editions of *MI* is the tardiness of appearance, and the annual cumulations have often lagged behind by several months. On the positive side, *The Music Index on CD-ROM* (1981-present) is updated annually and promises to provide the kind of access that will delight music lovers everywhere.

The *International Repertory of Music Literature* that is now issued under the title *Music Literature International* (1967-present) is published quarterly with the 4th issue each year being an annual cumulation. It is regarded as a major source of up-to-date information in the field of music bibliography, for it provides abstracts of books and journal articles, book reviews, dissertations, iconographies, catalogs, and much more.

Other bibliographies in this area can be traced through an important handbook entitled *The Humanities: A Selective Guide to Information Sources* by R. Blazek and E. Aversa (4th.ed.; 1994).

The Ministry of Education

Not to be ignored is the important ministry of education, necessitating a knowledge of biblical principles of education, the history of education, and modern research in the field of education. Information about some of the most important retrospective works can be obtained from *The Minister's Library.* And not to be forgotten are *ERIC (Educational Resources Information Center)* and *Education Abstracts*, both of which have been discussed in a previous chapter.

More focused is the work of DeWitte Campbell Wyckoff entitled *Suggested Bibliography in Christian Education for Seminary and College Libraries* (1968, with a supplement covering the years 1968--1993 released in 1995). This work is possibly the most extensive bibliography to be published in this area of the church's service.

Other reference works that are now dated include the *Bibliography of American Educational History* by Francesco Cordasco and William W. Brickman (1975), and the *Bibliographic Guide to Educational Research*, by Dorothea M. Berry (1975).

Ministry to Ethnic Groups

Ethnic NewsWatch, available via the Internet or CD-ROM, contains a full text database of the newspapers, magazines and journals of the ethnic minority and native press. Well over 100 publications are included. The coverage is comprehensive, incorporating local, national and global data. A wide range of subjects is covered, including art, biographies of prominent people, business, cultural diversity, education, environment, ethnic issues, health and medicine, history, multicultural issues, politics and government, science, sports and recreation, and urban issues. Articles, editorials, newspaper columns, reviews of books, movies, theater, and television programs, and much more are included. Searching the database is by keyword that provides the complete text of all articles.

The Ministry of Counseling

Most of the counseling bibliographies listed in the first edition of this book have not been brought up-to-date and are therefore seriously dated. A 30-volume set of books edited by Gary R. Collins called *Resources in Christian Counseling* is worth consulting. Each volume contains a valuable bibliography. The set was published between 1986--1991. Topics covered include innovative approaches to counseling, the counseling of Christian workers, prayer, eating disorders, depression, family violence and abuse, crisis counseling, guilt, the search for meaning, unplanned pregnancies and/or infertility, a lack of self-control, substance abuse, homosexuality, anger and aggression, demonic possession, marriage, divorce, AIDS, how to handle disabilities, sexual disorders, cognitive therapy techniques, conflict management, and the importance of high ethical standards in Christian counseling.

In 1992 the Association for Religious and Value Issues for Counseling issued *Counseling and Spiritual Values: A Bibliography*. This 170-page monograph ably fulfills the title by concentrating on counseling and the spiritual life.

Where the family is concerned, the two-volume work by the Wakefield Washington Associates, Inc., entitled *Family Research: A Source Book, Analysis, and Guide to Federal Funding* (1979) still retains some value. It is the outgrowth of years of sociological research and catalogs the kind of work being done by Federal agencies. It also is suggestive of many areas of investigation which doctoral students in D.Min. programs in marriage and family ministries might profitably bring up-to-date while adapting their findings to the local church.

As has been mentioned before, there are bibliographies on nearly every subject imaginable. They may be found in the catalog of your library or the *Library of Congress Catalog—Books: Subjects* or *Subject Guide to Books in Print*. The approved subject heading will be followed by a dash and the word bibliography:

MARRIAGE--BIBLIOGRAPHY

SINGLE ADULTS--BIBLIOGRAPHY

YOUTH--BIBLIOGRAPHY

Remember, a bibliography is supposed to be unbiased and list materials from all available sources.

LOOKING AHEAD

Good research should include information collected from books, periodicals, and unpublished materials. By checking *Dissertation Abstracts International* locate as many works as you can dealing with: (1) God's image in man, and (2) the theology of either Charles Gore, Soren Kierkegaard, or Paul Tillich. Take note of how each dissertation abstract has been prepared and the way in which each doctoral candidate has developed their theme.

15

Unpublished Materials

Competent research, of necessity, must demonstrate an awareness of the scholarly investigations of others. This does not mean that a term paper must cite dissertations in the footnotes and bibliography. It does mean that students submitting theses and dissertations for advanced degrees should know of, and have interacted with, the scholarly work of others.

Unpublished materials can include papers read at the meetings of different societies (e.g., the Evangelical Theological Society, the Society for New Testament Studies, or Society of Biblical Literature, etc.) that have not been made the material available in their respective journals. Such papers constitute a valuable resource and, in many instances, are included in the privately circulated proceedings of the society (e.g., proceedings of the annual meeting of the Christian Association for Psychological Studies or the American Theological Library Association, etc.).

Because such papers may be traced through an index or abstracting service such as *TREN* (Theological Research Exchange Network), that regularly microfilms and indexes unpublished theses and dissertations from about 70 cooperating theological institutions) this chapter will concentrate on dissertations. Researchers can search the *TREN* database from the TREN homepage [www.tren.com]. The database can be searched by author, title, school, and subject. Users can scan search results and print them on an order form, which can be mailed to TREN to purchase microfiche or print copies of theses and dissertations.

In the United States, we have excellent coverage of dissertations from 1861 (when the first doctorates were awarded by Yale University) to the present. By the turn of the century about 350 doctorates were awarded each year throughout the country. By 1950 the number had risen to about 6,000; in the 1970s the figure exceeded 35,000 annually; and the figure has continued to climb. With the introduction of professional doctorates (e.g., D.A., D.B.A., D.F.A., D.L.S., D.M.A., D.Min., D.Miss., D.Mus., D.S.W., etc.) an increase is inevitable.

Dissertations, and especially the bibliographies, can prove of inestimable value. The most useful source of finding dissertations on any subject is *Dissertation Abstracts International* (1861-present). *DAI* is published in three sections: Section A, Humanities and Social Sciences; Section B, Sciences and Engineering; and Section C, Worldwide. Bell & Howell Information and Learning (University Microfilms Inc.) he publisher of *DAI* estimates that between 95 to 98 per cent of doctoral dissertations written in the United States are included in *DAI*. *DAI* Sections A and B are published monthly, and Section C is published quarterly.

The easiest way to search *DAI* is through Internet subscription databases (e.g., *FirstSearch*, ProQuest, Ovid) or the CD-ROM version of *Dissertation Abstracts Ondisc*. The database can be searched by author, title, or keywords in all searchable fields. Retrieved records for doctoral dissertations (1980-present) include abstracts of about 350 words in length.

If electronic access to *DAI* is not available, the best way to search is by using the *Comprehensive Dissertation Index*. *CDI* is comprised of several sets of books. The main set of 37 volumes covers dissertations from 1861 to 1972. There are also a 38 volume, ten-year cumulation covering 1973 to 1982, and a 22 volume, five-year cumulation covering 1983 to 1987. For the years following these sets there are five-year supplements covering dissertations from the preceding years. Some libraries have only the five-year supplements beginning with 1973. Supplements are divided into three sections: Sciences, Social Sciences and humanities, and Authors. Searching is done by subject and author. When the desired records are found, the records give the volume and page number for the abstract in *DAI*.

American Doctoral Dissertations (1957-present) covers almost all doctoral dissertations from U.S. and Canadian institutions, and includes titles not abstracted by *DAI*. *ADD* is published annually and does not include abstracts.

Dissertations in progress may be traced through a journal entitled *Religious Studies Review* (1974-present) which regularly lists dissertation topics accepted for research.

Theses and dissertations submitted to universities overseas may also be traced by consulting the *Index to Theses Accepted for Higher Degrees in the Universities of Great Britain and Ireland* (1953-present); *Deutsche Nationalbibliographie und Bibliographie des im Ausland erschieneuen deutschsprachen Schriftums* (1968-present); *Jahresverzeichnis der deutschen Hochschulschriften 1885/86* (1887-1936 and 1937-present); and *Catalog des theses et ecris acadimeques, 1884/85* (1884-1952); et cetera.

* * * *

By the way of review, the process we have followed for the gathering of data began with (1) *general reference works*, followed by (2) *books*, then (3) *periodical articles*, and finally (4) *unpublished materials*. We have moved progressively from the general to the specific. Once you have mastered this approach and the diverse bibliographic sources available to you, there is nothing you should not be able to find.

Notes

1. Kodera, Atsushi, "MIT Chief Assesses Future Challenges," *The Daily Yomiuri (Tokyo)*, 25 January 1999, LEXIS-NEXIS Academic Universe, accessed 22 May 1999.

2. In 1 Corinthians 12:13 the Greek text reads *en*, and this preposition is usually translated "in, with, or by."

3. R. Glover, *Jesus in the Experience of Men* (London: Student Christian Movement, 1921), xiii.

4. C. S. Lewis, *Screwtape Letters* (New York: Macmillan Publishing Company, 1961), 128-29; see also C. S. Lewis, *God in the Dock*, ed. W. Hooper (Grand Rapids, MI: Wm. B. Eerdmanns, 1970), 200-01.

5. The theological significance of this purchase of a slave has been discussed by G. A. Deissmann in *Light from the Ancient East*, trans. L. R. M. Strahan, 4th ed.(New York: Harper & Brothers, 1927), 319-27.

6. *Letters from Mesopotamia*, trans. A.L. Oppenheim (Chicago: University of Chicago Press, 1967), 74-75.

7. J. von Allman, *Vocabulary of the Bible* (London: Lutterworth Press, 1958), 5.

8. X. Leon-Dufour, *Dictionary of Biblical Theology* (New York: Seabury Press, 1973), xvii.

9. C. Brown, ed., *The New International Dictionary of New Testament Theology*, Vol. 1 (Grand Rapids, MI: Zondervan Publishing House, 1975), 7. Copyright 1975 by Zondervan Publishing House. Used by permission of Zondervan Publishing House.

10. For a description of the theocracy (i.e., God ruling over the earth through His Chosen representatives) see J. D. Pentecost, *Things to Come* (Grand Rapids, MI: Zondervan Publishing House, 1958), 446-75. A theocratic approach to theology is theocentric, not anthropocentric, and should not be confused with the recent emergence of "reconstructionism" or "dominion theology."

11. J. D. Snider, *I Love Books* (Washington, DC: Review and Herald Publishing Company, 1942), 532.

12. Most of the Bible software packages that have proliferated in recent years include at least one searchable concordance. The most common is Strong's *Exhaustive Concordance*, which may also contain hypertext links to other online reference works such as lexicons or Bible dictionaries.

13. W. Barclay, *More New Testament Words* (New York: Harper and Row, 1958), v.

14. You may first use Young's *Analytical Concordance to the Bible* to identify the Hebrew and Greek words.

15. "Kittel" is better known in the literature as *TDNT*.

16. A decade later this student and the professor happened to meet at a wedding. Imagine the professor's surprise when his former student said, "Do you remember the course on bibliographic research that I took from you while in seminary? I was very unhappy with one assignment you gave us. Well, I've been in this pastorate for almost ten years, and I want you to know that the course was one of the most beneficial I took while in seminary. I think you will also be glad to know that I use word studies to liven up nearly all of my sermons. I find them indispensable when it comes to both illustrating and applying the thrust of a word or a passage."

17. Because this is an introduction to theological research, a lengthy discussion of the merits of philological research in Akkadian, Ugaritic, and Aramaic, et cetera, will not be undertaken. More advanced students may wish to consult Rosenthal's *Aramaic Handbook*; Wehr's *Arabic Dictionary*; the Assyrian Dictionary (CAD), published by the Oriental Institute of the University of Chicago; J. P. Smith's *Comprehensive Syriac Dictionary*; Moscati's *Introduction to the Comparative Grammar of the Semitic Languages*; Donner and Rollig's *Kanaanaische und Aramaische Inschriften*; Gordon's *Ugaritic Textbook*; and even

von Soden's *Akkadisches Handworterbuch*. Also of value is the *Dictionnaire des Inscriptions Semitiques de l'quest* by Jean and Hoftijzer.

18. C. H. Spurgeon, *Commenting and Commentaries* (New York: J. Carter, 1876), 1.

19. See articles in general encyclopedias or the art section of your public or academic library.

Index

The Authors

Cyril J. Barber has served as head librarian, Trinity Evangelical Divinity School (now a part of the Trinity International University); director of the library and associate professor of bibliography, Rosemead Graduate School of Psychology; and as professor of bibliography and dean of the Learning, Resources Center, Simon Greenleaf School of Law. He received an M.A.(L.S.) degree, *cum laude*, from the Rosary College Graduate School of Library and Information science, a M.Th. from Dallas Theological Seminary, and a D.Min., *magna cum laude*, from Talbot Theological Seminary. He is the author of more than 30 books and numerous journal articles, and has been awarded two *honoris causa* D.Litt. degrees. Now, in his retirement, he spends his time writing and speaking.

Robert M. Krauss, Jr., serves as the Serials/Public Services Librarian at Biola University. His areas of special interest are religious studies and bibliographic instruction in electronic databases and Internet research resources. A graduate of Talbot Theological Seminary (M.Div.), he served as an Air Force Chaplain for fourteen years, including three years as an instructor/course director at the Air Force Chaplain School and a tour of duty at the Pentagon as Chief of Air Force Family Programs. Prior to his theological training he served as an Air Force Instructor Pilot and was twice awarded the Distinguished Flying Cross for service in Vietnam. Krauss earned his M.A. in Marriage, Family and Child Counseling from the California Family Study Center, and a Master of Library and Information Science (M.L.I.S.) degree from the University of South Carolina.